THE NATURAL PATH TO
GENUINE LASTING HAPPINESS

THE NATURAL PATH TO GENUINE LASTING HAPPINESS

(As Shown by the Scientific Record of Life, by Psychology, by the Teachings of Great Religious and Humanitarian Leaders, and by Personal Experience)

BY

RODNEY GALE

VANTAGE PRESS

New York   Washington   Atlanta   Hollywood

Contents

(Section I is mostly paleontology and anthropology.)
(Section II is mostly anthropology and psychology.)
(Section III is mostly philosophy and religion.)
(Section IV is mostly sociology [social reform], with fur-
ther references to science, philosophy, psychology, and
religion.)

(The main point is that all these are interrelated; they fit
together. Solutions of major problems and increase of
well-being and happiness depend upon awareness of the
reality that runs through them all.)

Introduction

The way to find and experience deep, rich, lasting joy in life, here and now, can be described in both scientific and religious terms, and the two very different descriptions, having essentially the same meaning, are complementary approaches to the same basic reality. The requirement for genuine happiness is that you get nearer to that reality, get lined up with the universe. It involves simultaneously increasing understanding coupled with experience in closer, joy-bringing personal relations.

Science has always prided itself on getting close to understanding reality, but it usually misses the mark because of concentrating on only a small part of reality, abstracting from the whole just those tangible things that can be accurately measured, classified, catalogued, and experimented with, and forgetting the intangibles such as personal feelings and inspirations, which probably represent the more important part of reality, especially if you want to find true happiness. For that, you must get close to the whole of reality. The life sciences can do better in this respect than the physical sciences alone. Biology is a bridge between the physical sciences and the humanities, at least if the significant meaning can be recognized that runs through the long history of past life. Psychology could do much better than it usually does if it could keep from being continually thrown off the track by the distorted values and assumptions of modern society, which, though practically worldwide and thought to be realistic, are very far from being so.

The relevance of the religious approach can be readily seen as soon as it is explained that God is the Ultimate Reality of the universe, the fundamental truth, deeper than, though superficially obscured by, misleading appearances, misconceptions, and superstitions. Most religious people can be counted on to recognize that. Neither the most religious nor the least have any interest in a god who is unreal, or who is only a small part of reality. They can be joined in recognizing the importance of ultimate reality by those persons who consider themselves atheists and by all others in between. Everyone believes that something is real, and whatever he believes is most real is his god, no matter what he may say about it, whether it be the opportunity to make a pile of money, or the assemblage of physical forces visible around us, or something more worthy of the highest regard of a human being. Whether religious or irreligious, every person's concept is bound to be far from the actual reality. Everyone needs to work hard in the right direction (a direction, fortunately, that makes it become easier and pleasanter) to approach more closely to reality. Thus it is not a question of whether you believe in God or not, but of what is the nature of the god you do believe in.

Now for lasting happiness, it must be the actual Ultimate Reality that you get close to. It must be the real God. For this it is necessary to get beyond primitive and inadequate concepts of God. The anthropomorphic idea of a glorified old man in the sky is mostly what atheists do not believe in, and most other people nowadays have progressed beyond that stage. One point is often a stumbling block: it is difficult to make definite what personality can mean in connection with God. Certainly we should no longer attribute arbitrariness or favoritism to the real God. But there is bound to be a mystery about

Ultimate Reality, and perhaps we can get a better concept of the mystery if we couple together what we learn about the effects of *reality controlling the long history of life* with the realization that we can get closest to this reality by developing *deep, positive, personal relations* with other human beings. It is in such personal experiences that the personal aspect of God is to be discovered and understood, as will be more fully explained later.

The History of Life

Much more than is generally realized can be learned from the long evolutionary development of life. As a paleontologist I have studied and taught and thought about fossils for the major part of a lifetime. I have sought and, I believe, found the deeper meaning just mentioned back of these old shells, old bones, and other relics of the past. The process of evolutionary development has indeed been a very systematic one. It has been controlled through natural selection by the expression of reality in the surrounding environment.

In the course of geologic time, conditions are always changing. The changes force the life of the times to make adjustments. (Out of the many variations in characteristics of each kind of living creature, the ones that happen to go in the right directions are selected by the environment for survival.) The group (species) that makes the greatest biologic advance is very successful, multiplies greatly in numbers, and spreads widely over the world. The representatives of this group that reach each different biologic environment tend to adjust, by the same process, to that environment, so becoming different from each other and evolving into different species, even sometimes different genera or higher ranks in the biologic classification. This process is known as adaptive radiation, the diversifying characteristics spreading out in all directions like the radiating rays of the sun.

But the local adaptations require (or at least induce) specialization, which involves the sacrifice of other capacities to emphasize the specialty, and when new major changes occur in the environments, the specialists do not have enough other capacities left to make the new needed adjustments. They become extinct or retire to some out-of-the-way corner of the biologic economy (like the deep sea, where conditions change little and there is less competition), and where they may stagnate for untold ages indefinitely. In either case they are the failures of life, and there have been a great many of them, especially of those that have become extinct; indeed, many more than the lines that have survived.

But always there is some group that has remained in a varied environment and so has not specialized but has retained its all-round balance of capacities. It is most able to adjust to new conditions by making another real biologic advance, whereupon it becomes highly successful, multiplies greatly in numbers, and spreads widely over the earth in a new adaptive radiation. In each environment reached by its representatives they compete with the former occupants (often being for them the chief new factor in their changing environment, to which they cannot adjust), and the usual winning out of the new radiants provides objective evidence that they really have made a biologic advance. The winning out seldom involves direct conflict, but rather a greater ability to utilize available food supplies and other resources (including sunshine and water for plants), and a greater ability to avoid predators and cope with climatic and other hardships. They are the successes of life.

The most successful part of each radiation leads on to the next radiation and constitutes the *main line of evolutionary advance,* which eventually evolves into man. Besides the outstanding successes and the definite failures, there are of course a great many intermediate types that hang on and do fairly well, but are too restricted to be able to challenge the main line and can at best maintain themselves and possibly provide assistance to the main line, in the form of food or other useful contributions.

So we have in the record of life a practical index of the characteristics that lead to success and the characteristics that lead to failure. They contrast strikingly in two respects: (1) The main line has always maintained an all-round balanced development of capacities, instead of specializing; and (2) the main line has developed step by step to the highest levels of the times its sensitivity, awareness, alertness, and receptivity, in contrast to callousness, security, and rigidity. It is these features that have made it always more adaptable, and it is important to speak not merely of the adaptability but to go on further and to enumerate those more particular features that provide the adaptability. Moreover, it is quite unreasonable for us to continue to rely on qualities which have consistently led to failure or inferiority, during the 600 million years or more that we can see clearly, when we can much better put our trust in ones which have—for an equally long time—been the basis of success for the main line and can now be the key to happiness for the individual.

It is especially important to consider the nature of *receptivity,* which is the scientific equivalent of the religious term *humility* (or meekness) if properly understood, the basis of any truly religious attitude. It is openness, the ability to take in, freedom from previous commitments (for examples among lower creatures, see below), and for us freedom from prejudices, and a readiness to accept the new and/or the old on its merits.

A very early example of receptivity is provided by

the ancestral Coelenterates about a billion years ago, the group which gave rise to the later corals and their associates, and may also represent a stage along the main line. They invented a stomach, an organ for the more efficient reception and processing of food. Previously every cell in the body had to absorb and digest food for itself. The Coelenterates developed an interior hollow (*coel,* hollow; *enteron,* intestine; though the alimentary canal was not then differentiated between stomach and intestine) which could take in a charge of sea water. If it contained particles of material suitable for food, it would close the opening and secrete into the hollow a little hydrochloric acid and other juices, to start the digestive process before the cells lining the hollow would absorb the food and finish the digestion, passing some of the nutrient on to cells beyond. Whether the progressive main-line early members of this group had an opening (anus) at the rear end of the alimentary canal for the discharge of waste is not known, but the surviving branch-line members have to discharge through the intake opening, an unsanitary and inefficient makeshift.

The corals have forfeited a place on the main line, and so have been relegated to a series of branch lines, by becoming sessile—attached to the bottom—like a good many of their relatives, close and distant, with the result that they could no longer move around and be aware of a wider area, and thus also they had special difficulty in discharging waste. As the waste accumulating around them reacted with sea water and made a deposit of stony material, in the form of a cup or vase, it resulted in their committing themselves, like many others, to an encasing external skeleton (later utilized for support and security) that further reduced awareness of their immediate surroundings. The shell of a mollusk does the same. As for becoming sessile, the plants are another large group that, rooted to the spot, have also given up their opportunity to move around and see the world, even to the

4

extent that their very primitive Flagellate ancestors could, with their flagella and their pigmented "eye"-spots.

Other examples of receptivity will be given later, but first a very brief summary of the origin of life on the earth is needed. The evidence is very strong that at the time of the origin of life the atmosphere was composed mostly of poisonous gases (methane, ammonia, carbon monoxide and dioxide, and sulfur dioxide, hydrogen sulfide, and hydrogen), with probably some free nitrogen, but no free oxygen. It was a reducing atmosphere, in contrast to our present oxidizing one. If there had been any free oxygen, the first three gases named and some others (plus the exposed rocks) would have quickly combined with it and eliminated it as such. Our atmosphere then was more like the present atmospheres of other planets that have atmospheres. Surprisingly, that kind of atmosphere was more favorable for the origin of life than our present one would have been, and was probably even necessary for it. Under those conditions, with no protective layer of ozone in the upper atmosphere to filter the sun's rays, the sun beat down with severe intensity on shallow pools of water and converted some of the methane into higher hydrocarbons and, with other substances, into the so-called "organic" compounds needed for life. These included nearly all the amino acids, which are the building blocks of proteins; five- and six-carbon sugars; the four or five nitrogen bases needed to construct the nucleic acids; and the biologic source of chemical energy, ATP (adenosine triphosphate). Lightning was also a factor to help in this process. The production of these substances has been demonstrated in laboratory experiments simulating early conditions on the earth before the origin of life. In time they accumulated to produce what has been called an *inorganic soup.*

A colloid is a mass of very tiny particles dispersed in

a fluid medium. It may be made of particles of smoke, dust, mud, or very large molecules, such as were accumulating in the inorganic soup. The particles may have electrical charges, some positive, some negative. In a mixture of positive and negative particles, those with opposite charges tend to attract each other. If the opposites touch, they neutralize their charges and coagulate, but if they are kept from touching each other by protective films of water molecules adhering to each particle, they nevertheless attract each other without coagulating, and form little globular masses of still mobile but more concentrated materials called *co-acervates*. The inward pull on the outermost layer of each globule, with no opposing outward pull, tends to make an even more compact membrane-like crust around the globule.

Co-acervates have the capacity to attract and absorb materials from the surrounding medium, concentrating them; and chemical reactions may take place within, resulting in the production of some products that are constructive and others that are repulsed and expelled as wastes, thus making a *through-flowing chemical system*. A globule may grow until it becomes unstable because of its size, and then divide into two. These processes also have been observed in the laboratory. There are, in addition, a number of other ways in which concentrations may have been effected.

The really critical point for the origin of life was the organization of the first minimum sequence of effective self-replicating nucleic acid (RNA, ribonucleic acid, or DNA, deoxyribonucleic acid). These are composed of five-carbon sugars joined at the side to nitrogen bases (the combination, one of each, called a nucleoside), and these tied by a phosphate unit to make a complete link (nucleotide) in the long-chain molecule of nucleic acid. All of these parts were present in the inorganic soup. ATP probably supplied the energy needed to unite them, though it is not understood just how this was done (for it requires the removal of water, with water molecules all around). The order or sequence of the four types of nucleosides in the long chain determines the hereditary characteristics of the cell. This can reproduce itself, for each nitrogen base automatically attracts from the surrounding medium its complementary base until a parallel chain forms next to the original one. This, in turn, after they are separated, forms next to it one just like the original. The order or sequence of the nucleosides also controls the production of proteins within the cell, which (as enzymes) regulate the chemical processes that go on, determining the characteristics of the cell and of the creature. Presumably, not all the refinements of advanced cells would be needed at the start. With many millions of tiny laboratories all over the world experimenting for millions of years with different sequences, it seems that sooner or later a sequence would be hit upon in the right environment to provide the chemical control needed to keep the process going, and then we had life. It probably included forming a more effective cell membrane, and eventually the chains were extended to provide control for the chemical reactions needed to utilize outside sources of energy to recharge the ATP batteries, beginning with the simplest ferments, which break down six-carbon sugars and other naturally occurring substances.

Life may have started more than once and used up all the inorganic soup before the final successful start. After that, it was unlikely that any new start could compete with the forms already established. The biologic unity of all life indicates that it did not. The earliest type probably should be classified as the simplest, tiniest form of bacteria, no bigger than a virus. Viruses are degenerate bacteria, and can live only as parasites in the cells of other organisms. Blue-green "algae" are merely bacteria that have developed the ability to utilize chlorophyll (the green, *chlor,* material in the leaves, *phyll,* and other parts of plants and primitive organisms) in order to take in energy from sunlight and build organic materials by photosynthesis. Blue-green "algae" are so much simpler than true *Algae* that they should not be thought of together. They have been identified in rocks more than three billion years old. They multiplied in great numbers in both marine and non-marine environments, and worked practically alone for probably two billion years giving off oxygen during photosynthesis, which oxidized the atmosphere and the surface rocks and produced a new atmosphere with free oxygen. After that they have been joined in this task by the true *Algae,* and still later by mosses and land plants. Even in these higher organisms, however, it may still be the blue-green "algae" that are doing it, for the chlorophyll in the more advanced cells is all concentrated in chloroplasts, which are tiny organisms reproducing themselves within the larger cells as if they were blue-green "algae" that had long ago joined the higher organisms in symbiosis (just as a lichen is a symbiotic combination of a fungus and a blue-green "alga" or a true green alga). Another kind of bacterium seems also to have joined symbiotically within the cells of all higher organisms to help with the energy restoration of ATP (in the form of mitochondria).

If it were not for the chlorophyll-bearing organisms today continuously replenishing the free oxygen, it would be quickly used up; in about 1500 years, it has been estimated. Thus, one of the best indications of life in other parts of the universe would be the occurrence of free oxygen in abundance, if it could be distinguished from combined oxygen at great distances. Only after the oxygen in the atmosphere had built up to a sufficient level could the higher bacteria switch over to the much more efficient oxygen metabolism for getting their energy, and then all other forms of life utilizing it could begin. That was when evolutionary development speeded up rapidly.

Bacteria, viruses, and blue-green "algae" are very much simpler organisms than all other forms of life. They have no nucleus in the cell to hold together the hereditary and directive chains of nucleic acid and so are called prokaryotes (*pro,* before; *karyon,* nucleus). The eukaryotes (*eu,* proper), from the Flagellates on, are very much more advanced. They have their multiple chromosomes organized within the nucleus so that all of their characteristics can be passed on accurately in the reproduction of cells by the complex mechanisms of meiosis and mitosis, which are found in all the rest of the primitive creatures and in all plants and animals. The Flagellates are the last group ancestral to all these other organisms. Some Flagellates have chlorophyll and lead on toward *Algae* and plants; others lack it and lead on toward more animal-like *Protozoa,* sponges, and animals. Though some of the higher bacteria can voluntarily move about a little, the Flagellates can do it much better with their fully developed whip-like flagella and the localized sensitivity of their "eye"-spots that can distinguish between light and dark. Other advances made at this stage include sexual differentiation and in a few cases cooperation of cells to make multicelluar organisms. The *Algae* differ from the *Flagellata* only in that their classes are dominated by members which have a main sessile stage in their life cycles, whereas in the Flagellate groups most of the members are free at all times. The main line Flagellates evolved directly into the first truly animal level of development, which may have been a more or less tubular multicellular organism (metazoan), from which came the Coelenterates already described.

As time went on, all kinds of sensitivity and receptivity increased. At a somewhat later time, about 700 million years ago, the very early members of the group of Nemertine (or ribbon) worms provide another illustration of the development of main-line characteristics.

FLAGELLATES.

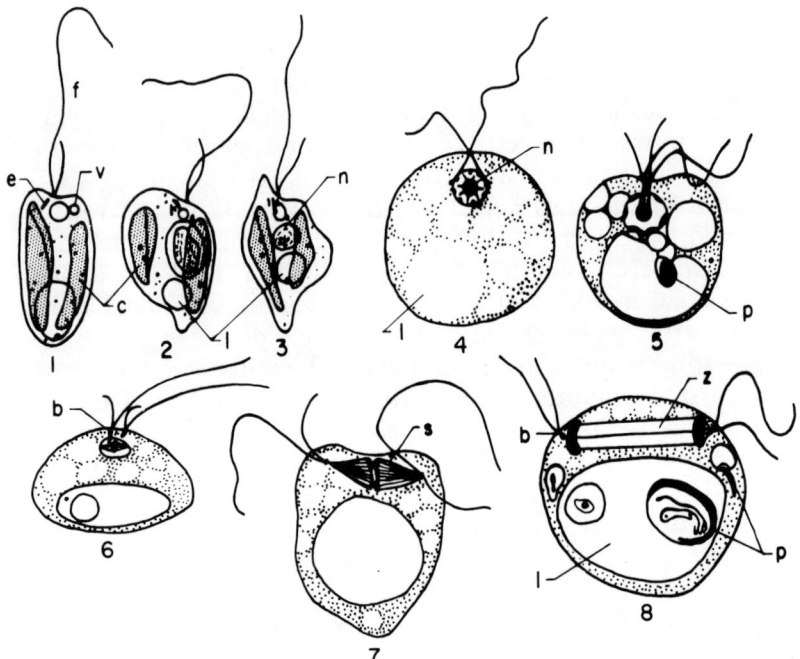

1–3 *Ochromonas mutabilis* Klebs showing changeable shape (after W. Conrad); 4–8 *O. granularis* Doflein showing stages in nucleic division (after F. Doflein): b, basal granule (centrosome); c, chromatophore; e, eye spot (stigma) - Figs. 2 and 3 have three stigmata; f, flagellum; l, leucosin globule; n, nucleus; p, particle of food being absorbed; s, mitotic spindle; v, contractile vacuoles; z, spindle drawn out into a cylinder prior to cell separation (from *Archiv für Protistenkunde*, vols. 44 and 56, used by permission of Gustav Fischer, Jena 69). Redrawn by Mary Douglass, magnification approximately 1500 times.

Ochromonas is a genus of Chrysomonad Flagellates which may be somewhat like the ancestral main-line Proto-Flagellates of the Proterozoic about a billion years ago. They are very versatile, inhabiting both fresh and marine waters. They have a flexible surface membrane which allows them to change shape freely. Extrusions of protoplasm enable them to absorb particles of food, as does an amoeba, and pull them in through

They added a third zone of multiplying cells between the outer and inner coatings so that the body could grow thicker and provide for muscles and other interior structures; and, for nourishing the thicker interior, a somewhat watery circulating system, but even then with some red blood (haemoglobin) cells; and a very primitive drainage (kidney) system to carry out waste from the interior, in addition to an anus at the end of the alimentary canal. Some immediate descendants of a group such as this then became receptive to a new source of food in the form of particles washed down in the deltas of rivers, gaining the ability to swim against the currents with their mouths open, sieving out the food particles, and discharging the sea water through gill slits. Later the gills, exposed to this current, became especially receptive

---

intake vacuoles, discharging waste through usually smaller contractile vacuoles. Thus they can acquire energy like an animal, but they can also do it like a plant, for they engage in photosynthesis with the help of chlorophyll kept in bodies within the cell, known as chromatophores. Some species have only reduced or pale-colored chromatophores, and grade into the closely related colorless genus *Monas*, which is entirely animal-like in its metabolism. These genera store nutriment in the form of the albumin leucosin instead of the starch characteristic of other classes of Flagellates. They have brownish-red spots or streaks that are sensitive to light, the "eye"-spots or stigmata. The longer of the two unequal flagella can pull them forward by its movement; the shorter is believed to cause rotary motion. As part of the reproductive process they sometimes secrete spherical internal siliceous cysts, believed to be of sexual origin, around the important constituents of the cell, but in the related genus *Ochrosphaera*, which produces recognizable gametes with "eye"-spots otherwise resembling zoospores, there are no cysts; the gametes simply fuse and the meiotic reduction follows immediately after. Also, some species of *Ochromonas* and related genera can develop into colonies of a number of individuals, while more distantly related Flagellates, such as *Volvox*, can organize the cells into a single multicellular unit with division of labor or function among the cells. It seems likely that all eukaryotic life evolved from a type not very different from *Ochromonas*.

11

A NEMERTINE WORM.

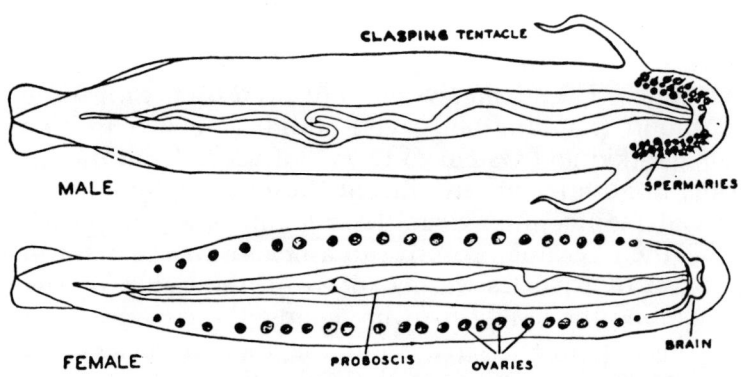

CLASPING TENTACLE

MALE

SPERMARIES

FEMALE   PROBOSCIS   OVARIES   BRAIN

Sexual dimorphism in *Nectonemertes mirabilis*, after Wesley R. Coe, Scripps Inst. Oceanography, Univ. of Calif., La Jolla, Bull. Vol. 6, shown approximately half natural size.

Deep-sea *Nemertea* (Nemertine worms), like other deep-sea creatures, often preserve in their unchanging environment some of the features of very ancient stages of development. *Necto* means *swimming*. The form shown in the diagram uses its tail fins as well as the undulatory motion of its body for swimming. Near-shore *Nemertea* have more sense organs. Some have larger brain nerve centers at the back of the head, and in the *Paleonemertea* these connect with the nerve that runs down the center of the back outside of the circular muscles. Some have many pairs of paired side branches from the intestine, pairs of ovaries and pairs of kidney canals, showing the beginnings of segmentation. It seems likely that in some ancient forms intestinal branches near the front end could have broken through by way of genital pores, kidney canals, or otherwise to make gill slits, such as are characteristic of primitive Chordates and Vertebrates. The long muscular proboscis that could be darted forward to capture prey is a specialization probably not present in ancient mainline representatives, but its sheath was in a position to develop into the notochord of primitive Chordates and the backbone of Vertebrates. Some species develop through a pilidium-type larva similar to the embryonic stages of many higher groups.

to the absorption of oxygen. At about this stage of food-sifting they developed a coelom—an additional body cavity between the alimentary tract and the outer body wall. It serves to separate the two walls so that each can perform its different functions separately without interfering with the other, one adapting to the inner world, the other to the outer. It occurs in all higher animals.

Later, as these food-sifting coelomates approached the state of very primitive Chordates (the beginning of the large group, or phylum, of creatures to which we belong) they made further advances. In order to wriggle and swim better against the currents they developed segmentation, so that muscles could pull alternatingly in opposite directions, and they acquired a strengthening rod (the notochord) down their backs for the muscles to pull against. In the course of time this notochord evolved into the vertebral column of all higher animals; a heart also developed to provide more efficient circulation of blood and generate extra energy for a more active life. Since their backs were in contact with the surface of the water, they tended to emphasize the part of their nervous system that went along their backs, and it became associated with the vertebral column. All this was directed by a three-part brain with a basic structure corresponding to our own. Thus they gradually made the transition to fresh water environments, which also involved a drastic revision of their kidneys.

While these main line creatures were making the transition toward becoming vertebrates, they were still required to go back to the sea to lay their eggs so that the young would grow up in the old environment until they could develop capacities needed to cope with the new. It was then that the rest of the invertebrates dropped off, including the lower Chordates (Amphioxus, the Tunicates, and perhaps the acorn worms, *Balanoglossus*, etc., and the colonial Pterobranchs). Most of the higher invertebrates (mollusks, segmented worms, Arthropods, even Echinoderms and the less familiar Brachiopods and

Bryozoa) show relics of the advanced characteristics, such as segmentation and hearts, but these have degenerated as the non-progressive branches of the radiation mostly became sessile and/or encased themselves in armor, and so declined in awareness of the surrounding world. Many also sacrificed their capacities in order to become parasitic or to emphasize predatory specialties. Because many descended to live on or near the sea bottom, near shore, they tended to develop the underneath parts of their nervous systems to a greater degree to guide them in relation to the diversities of that bottom. Later only a few made the difficult transitions to fresh water independently—and some even to land and air environments (only the insects in the last).

Diagrammatic representation of all these relationships is shown on the accompanying chart.

After that the record becomes still clearer. About 400 million years ago, the very earliest of the bony fishes (the *Crossopterygii*, or fringe-finned fishes—*crosso*, fringe, *pter*, fin or wing) developed lungs to help them get from stagnant fresh-water pools in rivers drying up to other pools not so stagnant. For these overland excursions they also developed two pairs of paired fins in the positions of the limbs of land quadrupeds, strengthened by internal bony axes, the bones corresponding in number and position, function and shape to the bones in the limbs of all higher vertebrates, including ourselves; and the shoulder girdle and upper part of the backbone became bony too, and were thus strengthened. In addition, they acquired connections (choanae) between the nostrils and the throat for better gasping for air in the stagnant pools, and so their sense of smell also improved. They developed more efficient jaws braced against new braincases; and surface skin scales migrated into the mouth to become teeth (sharp, conical teeth, with many labyrinthine infoldings of enamel).

It must be remembered that all these changes were

14

CROSSOPTERYGIANS.

A. The Devonian Crossopterygian, *Eusthenopteron foordi,* from the Upper Devonian beds near Escuminac, Quebec. Actual length of the fish about two feet. A model by George G. Simpson, made before the living species was known. From *Historical Geology* by Carl O. Dunbar, used by permission of Prof. Dunbar and John Wiley & Sons.

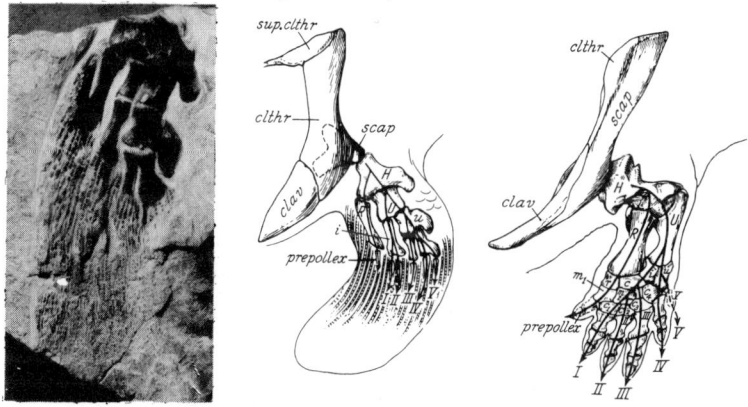

B. Resemblances between a Crossopterygian fin and the limb of a primitive land animal. Left, unretouched photograph of the left front fin of *Eusthenopteron foordi*; center, diagram of the skeletal elements of the same fin, with the flexible outer portions curved to the left to show correspondence with the amphibian; right, the corresponding limb of a late Paleozoic amphibian, *Eryops.* H, humerus; R, radius; U, ulna; u, ulnare; i, intermedium; r, radiale; c, centrale. Photograph by permission of the Buffalo Museum of Science, Buffalo, New York. Diagrams after W. K. Gregory, American Museum of Natural History.

C. The Living Species *Latimeria chalumnae* J. L. B. Smith, Museum, East London, South Africa

accomplished by natural selection under the guidance of the surrounding reality in the environment, for those individuals which did not happen to have variations in the right directions survived in smaller numbers, if at all, and so passed their characteristics on to few, if any, offspring. The branch lines of this radiation that went into permanently flowing rivers or lakes or back to the ocean had no need for lungs, and so converted them into swim bladders for hydrostatic balancing purposes. Among them are the fish we get for dinner in the restaurant. Some, like the salmon, still have to go back to fresh water to lay their eggs, so that their young can grow up in the environment of their origin.

But the land explorers began to linger on the land to catch the wingless insects they found there, needing only to return to the water to lay their eggs, and so became amphibians (Labyrinthodonts, from which descended the unprogressive frogs and salamanders and many early fossil types that became extinct, as well as the higher vertebrates). Eventually the eggs of some developed an enclosing membrane (or amnion) and other

16

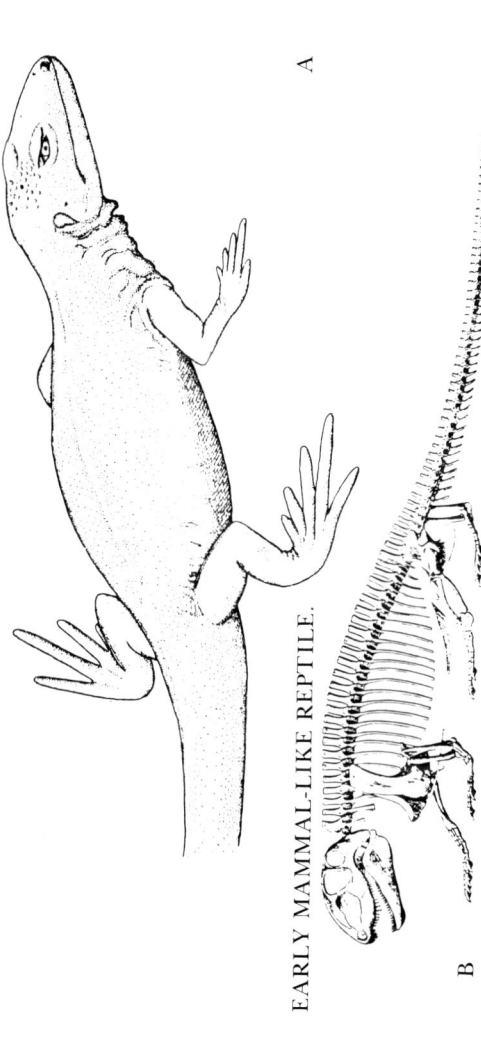

EARLY MAMMAL-LIKE REPTILE.

A

B

A. *Gephyrostegus bohemicus.* Restoration of adult by Robert L. Carroll. An Anthracosaurian amphibian from mid-Pennsylvanian age of Czechoslovakia, a survival from a probable mid-Mississippian stage of development appropriate for ancestry of reptiles in upper Mississippian. It was related to *Diplovertebron,* which (as the name indicates) had double vertebrae, with the amphibian-type vertebra being replaced by a more advanced type (from *Handbuch der Paläoherpetologie,* Vol. 5B, 1972, used by permission of Gustav Fischer, Stuttgart 72).

B. Skeletal restoration of *Haptodus* A Sphenacodont Pelycosaur from the lowest Permian near Dresden, Germany, which, like the Pennsylvanian *Macromerion* of Central Europe, is probably a hold-over from a very early mammal-like reptile stage. *H. (Pantelosaurus) saxonicus,* about thirteen percent of natural size. Modified from Von Huene's figures and data. Length, as restored from the largest known specimen, about 140 cm. (From the Geological Society of America, Special Paper 28, by Alfred S. Romer and L. I. Price.)

important features that kept them from drying out and enabled them to be laid on land (a safer place, by the way, for at that time there was not much else on the land to bother them). These transitions probably took place in the region of Greenland, Scotland, and Nova Scotia, which in those days were next to each other, before the continents separated. Soon after that they turned into the mammal-like reptiles or reptile-like mammals (*Synapsida*) and the sub-reptiles, some migrating southwestward into Texas and some southeastward through Europe to South Africa, the core of the southern hemisphere continent of Gondwanaland. The sub-reptiles (*Anapsida*), very abundant and varied in those early times, were represented by Cotylosaurs (*saur,* reptile; and *cotyle,* indicating the cup-like hollows in both ends of their vertebrae), and perhaps by most of the various later seagoing types; but they are represented today only by the still archaic turtles and tortoises.

The reptile-like mammals were almost certainly as early as the sub-reptiles, appearing in the same beds as the earliest sub-reptiles. Those of the less advanced Pelycosaur division were more like reptiles, but the ones that went to South Africa and found themselves around the edges of the expanding glaciation of Upper Pennsylvanian time (about 275 million years ago) most probably developed warm-bloodedness, in response to the glacial conditions there, and other progressive features, becoming more like mammals (the division *Therapsida, ther,* beast or mammal; and *apse,* bridge, referring to the bony connections between the holes in the outer skull, which were more mammal-like).

They sent representatives to Europe and North America, and when conditions first became favorable for their preservation in South Africa, they are revealed there in such great variety that their development is often referred to as an explosive radiation. That is indicative of a major biologic advance. Some of the most progressive—the dog-toothed, dog-jawed division and

18

their ancestors—developed a partition in the roof of the mouth, called a secondary palate, which separated the air current between the nose and the throat from the mouth, so that they could eat and breathe at the same time—an indication of warm-bloodedness, which requires more continuous breathing. Most probably this developed among the ancestral members first in the form of soft tissues, and thus could not be preserved in fossils until they were later strengthened by bone. There were many other mammal-like features such as, for instance, the count of the joints in the toes and the double knobs in the back of the skull for articulation with the spine (double occipital condyles), and the further development of the bony inner braincase to replace the old outer covering that had been drawn out into a series of holes, with bridges between them, by the pull of muscles. They also reduced the number of bones in the jaw until there was just one little one besides the single large dentary bone of mammals. During the arid times that followed the glaciation, the main line of Therapsids went on toward the development of the very advanced mammalian type of kidney for conserving moisture, while the true reptiles (*Diapsida*) and their derivatives, the birds, developed the very different uric acid system, so that they could secrete waste in the form of a paste, with very little moisture.

The tremendous significance of the stepped up sensitivity of warm blood, with temperature control, should not be overlooked. As the glaciers advanced, natural selection selected the creatures with more warmth in their bodies for survival. They would huddle together in sheltered places and help keep each other warm, and the warmth in the other fellow's body felt good. Thus they grew to like each other, and affection developed on the earth, probably 275 million years ago. Of course, sexual attraction was a factor in it, too, being effective even farther back, but the new warmth made its influence last and raised it to a new high level.

THE BEGINNING OF AFFECTION.

Reconstruction of a scene during the Upper Pennsylvanian-age glaciation in South Africa, showing a group of Therapsids huddled together for warmth in a sheltered place, with some of the vegetation of

From that time on cooperation within the group, mother love, and care for the young characterize the successful warm-blooded descendants. The change would be just as significant if it happened at a somewhat later time, but there is no evidence of an effective cause at a later time, and that, coupled with the positive evidence of the secondary palate, the explosive radiation, and the last point of common ancestry of the two warm-blooded groups—the birds and mammals—make it probable that it occurred then. There are some other minor kinds of evidence for it, too. Probably the early true reptiles, the early Archosaurs (ancestors of the dinosaurs, flying reptiles, and crocodiles) and even the ancestors of the other modern true reptiles (not including the turtles) had some of the warmth also, for the birds split off from the dinosaurs after they and the other reptiles had developed the uric acid kidneys; but most of the reptiles adopted less active ways of living or resorted to consistently warm tropical regions, and so did not keep up the energy level that warm blood requires. Almost certainly the flying reptiles, the Pterosaurs, which, like the birds, are really flying dinosaurs, had to keep up that energy level, and maybe the dinosaurs did too, at least to some extent, to move their great bodies around. But the crocodiles, lizards, and snakes didn't need it. Only the crocodiles kept the secondary palate for breathing nearly under water, and the birds and the Pterosaurs moved their nostrils far back instead, to accomplish the same purpose for which the secondary pallate was originally developed. The true reptiles also made other changes, differing from mammals, including a different formula for joints in the toes and a single occipital condyle.

The scene during the great middle era of life (the Mesozoic) is very instructive for understanding life relationships. Dinosaurs and other reptiles and sub-reptiles

A. *Cistecephalus planiceps* Owen. A Dicynodont vegetarian Therapsid from the Upper Permian of South Africa. (From *Sitzungsber. Bayerische Akadamie Wiss. München*, 1935, pt. I, p. 17, after Broili and Schröder.) Approximately three-fourths natural size, redrawn by Cathy Hill.

B. *Watsoniella breviceps* Broili and Schröder. A Bauriamorph carnivorous Therapsid from the Lower Triassic of South Africa. (From the same p. 33.) Approximately three-fourths natural size, redrawn by Cathy Hill.

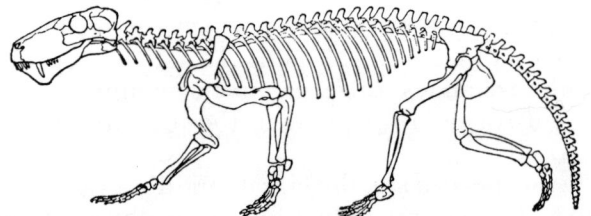

C. *Lycaenops*, a Gorgonopsian carnivorous Therapsid from the Upper Permian of South Africa (after A. S. Romer, 1967, size reduced).

The three Therapsids, while not directly on the main line, show the diversity of the group.

dominated the land, the swamps, the seas, and even the skies. If the so-called practical materialist of today could have viewed that scene in its time, he would have been reassured that success lies in size, physical strength, and ruthless competition. The mammals of that time were small, most of them no larger than a squirrel or tree-shrew, but they had warm fur, sensitive whiskers, and keen awareness; and they scurried around among the branches and in the shadows of the forest and kept from being stepped on by the huge reptiles. Would the "practical" materialist have thought that *they* would inherit the earth? Yet when continental uplifts at the end of the Mesozoic restricted the shallow seas, dried up the swamps, reduced the growth of lush vegetation, and limited the number of vegetarian dinosaurs and other vegetarian reptiles, the carnivorous predators ate up the remainder and, having no adequate food left for themselves, also became extinct. Then the mammals moved in and took their places and the meek inherited the earth, for the meek are those which have inner strength and versatility, an all-round balanced development of capacities, and greater sensitivity, awareness, and receptivity, so that they are more alert than vegetarians but do not have to use outer strength or the diabolical strategies of specialized predators in order to maintain themselves. This is not exceptional but the typical pattern of the development of life, occurring continuously throughout its history. The wonder is not that the great reptiles became extinct, in view of their tiny brains and deficient positive feeling capacities, but rather that they didn't become extinct sooner.

The main line mammals of the mid-Mesozoic, known as *Pantotheria* (generalized beasts) are among the earliest that customarily have been classified technically as mammals because of their single jawbones. They evolved on into the earliest Primates toward the end of the Mesozoic. The latter became somewhat like modern tarsiers but without their specializations, placing em-

23

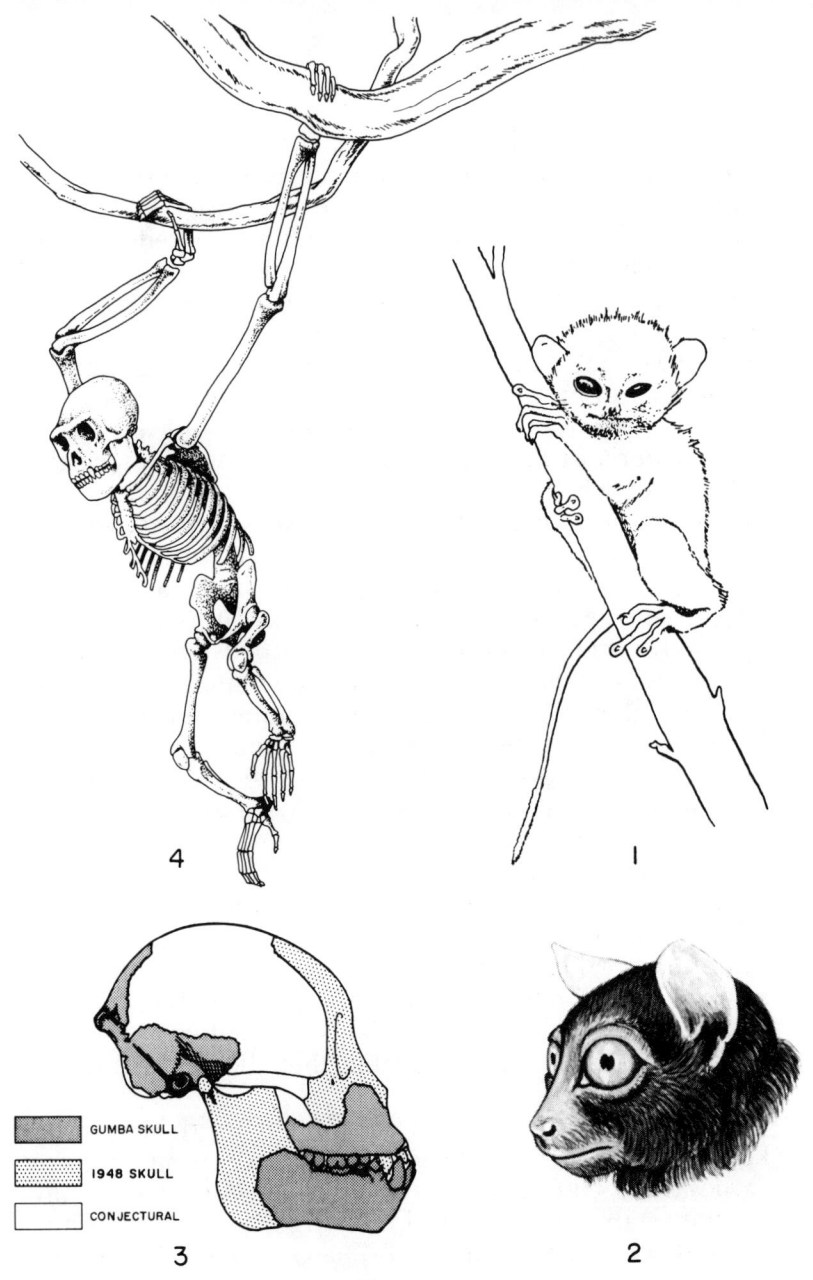

GUMBA SKULL
1948 SKULL
CONJECTURAL

4

1

3

2

phasis on vision, focusing the two eyes together (though not yet with complete bifocal vision) and shortening the snout, developing the grasping hand, etc. Other mammals radiated into the many divisions we know today (and some others): insectivores, bats, carnivores, whales, rodents, rabbits, edentates, and the many kinds of hoofed animals (ungulates). Some of these grew to a large size, and many repeated the other mistakes of the reptiles (specializing, and other developments that interfere with sensitivity and receptivity).

PRIMATES SIGNIFICANT FOR EARLY HISTORY
Explanations of Diagrams

1. Young of the modern tarsier, suggesting (except for specializations of hands and feet) what the main line was like in the early Eocene (after a drawing by W. E. LeGros Clark, in *Early Forerunners of Man*, 1934, by permission of Baillière Tindall, London).

2. *Necrolemur antiquus*, a middle Eocene progressive Tarsioid from France, probably not far from the main line but beginning to show specializations of the teeth and apparently fusion of the hind limb bones as in the modern tarsier. Reconstruction of the possible facial appearance. (Courtesy of Elwyn L. Simons, as in *Primate Evolution*, The Macmillan Co., p. 165, copyright ©, 1972).

3. *Proconsul africanus* Hopwood, a middle Miocene Anthropoid ape from East Africa, only a little removed from the main line in the direction of the apes, showing somewhat projecting canine teeth but not yet heavy brows or simian shelf, reconstruction from two skulls by P. R. Davis and John Napier in *Folia Primatologica*, Vol. 1, 1963, used by permission of S. Karger, Basel, Switzerland. Redrawn by Mary Douglass.

4. *Oreopithecus bambolii* Gervais, an uppermost Miocene Anthropoid from Italy that lived in the trees of a swamp environment but also apparently walked upright on the ground as shown by its pelvis and the stoutness and shape of the leg bones, and with man-like features of jaw and teeth, etc. Reconstruction by Elwyn L. Simons in his "Early Relatives of Man," in the *Scientific American* for July, 1964, copyright © 1964 by Scientific American, Inc. All rights reserved.

25

By about 40 million years ago the higher Primates or *Anthropoidea* (monkeys, apes, and the ancestors of men) appeared, with true bifocal vision. The ancestors of men deemphasized the projecting canine teeth (which had originated with the early main line mammal-like reptiles), in order to engage in more rotary chewing motions, and somewhere around 10 million years ago began to take a more upright position, freeing the hands for carrying implements, spending a lot of time on the ground, and probably resorting to the trees only for safety in emergencies and for relaxation. *Ramapithecus* was distributed across southern Asia and northeast Africa and perhaps Europe (the divine "ape," from *Rama,* the Indian god, and *pithecus,* ape, though the name is really a misnomer, since he should be thought of not as an ape but as a hominoid ancestor of men, and he was not divine unless the term is used in a very broad sense to indicate that he was the highest product of Ultimate Reality at that time, so far as we know). He had a short jaw and hence a more nearly vertical face. Besides a few teeth in Europe ascribed to *Ramapithecus,* there was another form mainly in Italy, and also in southwest Russia and northeast Africa, that may be related, known as *Oreopithecus* (the "ape" with the mountain-like, *oreo,* bumps on his teeth). He was more completely preserved but somewhat off the main line. He shows, however, the upright posture and nearly vertical face. It is reasonable to expect that if he attained an upright or near upright posture, the main line representatives of the time would have also.

From whatever favorable locality men may have first developed, some of them went into, or farther into Africa, some into, or farther into Asia, and also almost certainly some into, or farther into Europe, slowly progressing in each of these three regions more or less independently, and beginning to make very primitive stone tools to supplement the wooden ones they probably used

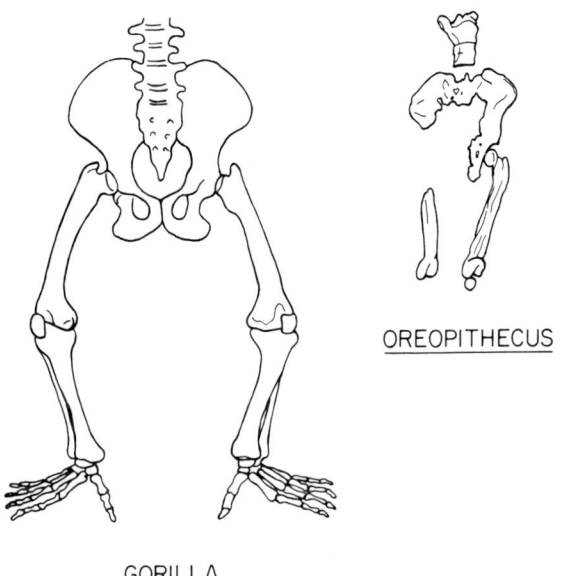

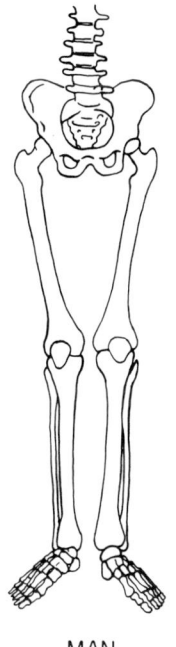

OREOPITHECUS

GORILLA

MAN

Hip and leg portions of gorilla, Oreopithecus, and man, after Wm. W. Howells in the *Evolution of the Genus Homo* (by permission of the Cummings Publishing Co. of Palo Alto, California, which has taken over this series from Addison-Wesley).

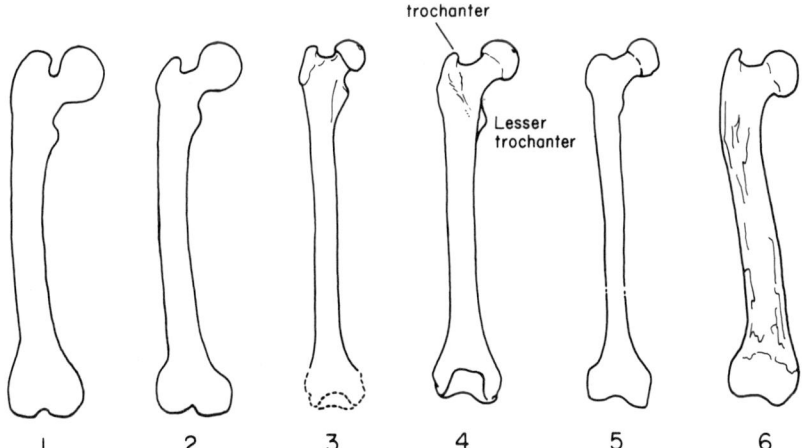

Upper leg bones (femora) of higher Anthropoids, converted to comparable lengths: 1) Gorilla; 2) Chimpanzee; 3) *Proconsul*; 4) modern man; 5) very early man, KNM-ER 1481 from East Rudolf, East Africa; 6) *Oreopithecus*. Nos. 1, 2, and 6 after A. H. Schultz; nos. 3 and 4 after Bernard Campbell; no. 5 from *Nature*, Vol. 242, April 13, 1973, p. 450. All figures redrawn by Mary Douglass.

at first. Under the influence of the changing climates of the latest series of glaciations, at least some of these groups became more active, seeking more nourishing food, cooperating and communicating in hunting, in gathering, preparing, and sharing food, and in other activities; and as a consequence their brains were of still greater assistance to them so that natural selection could promote the rapid increase in their brain size.

Two or three early types of men or near-men developed in or migrated into Africa. One type known as *Paranthropus* (*para,* along side of or parallel to; *anthropos,* man) did not attain a much larger brain size than modern apes, or a much larger brain size and degree of upright posture than can be presumed to have been reached 10 million years ago by some of the group of ancestral higher Primates and their close relatives which had inhabited India, southern China, east Africa, and Italy. The hand of *Paranthropus* had an imperfect grasping grip; likewise he had an imperfect adaptation to upright walking, and he apparently concentrated on tough vegetable food that caused him to develop heavy grinding teeth, a heavy, deep jaw, and strong jaw muscles, the pull of which on the low skull vault often produced a sagittal ridge running front to back along the top, and heavy, bony brows above the eyes. Another type, *Australopithecus* (*australo,* southern, from South Africa, the southern "ape") was probably related but had a smaller, lighter body build and teeth that enlarged to the rear less than in *Paranthropus,* and was probably adapted to a more varied diet in a more open, less forested area; but he still had a small brain, deep jaw, and skull roof that rose little above the level of the sharp protruding brows. Both these types probably utilized implements such as bones and naturally occurring stones, but the evidence is doubtful that they did appreciably more to fashion or improve tools than do chimpanzees and other animals.

A more progressive type, probably more closely related to man, that can be distinguished under the name *Telanthropus* (*tele,* complete, the full man) had a larger brain, a larger brain to body ratio, more arching skull, a lighter jaw, better adaptation to upright walking, more skillful hands (hence the species name *T. habilis,* skillful), and was undoubtedly the maker of stone tools that were not merely just the crude beginnings of tools but had recognizable style and symmetry. Although more commonly found in East Africa (at Lake Rudolf and Olduvai Gorge, etc.) this type appears also in South Africa with its tools, overlapping the Australopiths for a moderate space of time before the latter disappeared. Their tool culture is called, after Olduvai, Oldowan.

The branch of men that went to far eastern Asia developed early larger brains than most of the early southern Africans, and had molar teeth that got smaller toward the rear, more as in moderns, but the front parts of their skulls were narrow behind the solid brows, with the expansion toward the rear, and the bone was heavier on the average than in any other group, though some of the skull bones of the *Paranthropus* type were comparable. They long were known as *Pithecanthropus erectus* (the ape-man that stood erect), though later custom has tended to include them in the modern genus as *Homo erectus.* This is not a matter of right and wrong, but of convenience. There are so many different forms of this type from different parts of its long time range and wide geographic distribution that there may be several different species involved, or at least varieties, and it may well be more convenient to group them all under the old genus name *Pithecanthropus,* to distinguish them clearly from the early and late members of the modern genus *Homo.* They come from widely different ages in Java and from near Peking and other parts of China. Their rather crude chopper-chopping tool cultures are spread all over eastern Asia, except in the extreme north, and lasted until very late times, until the appear-

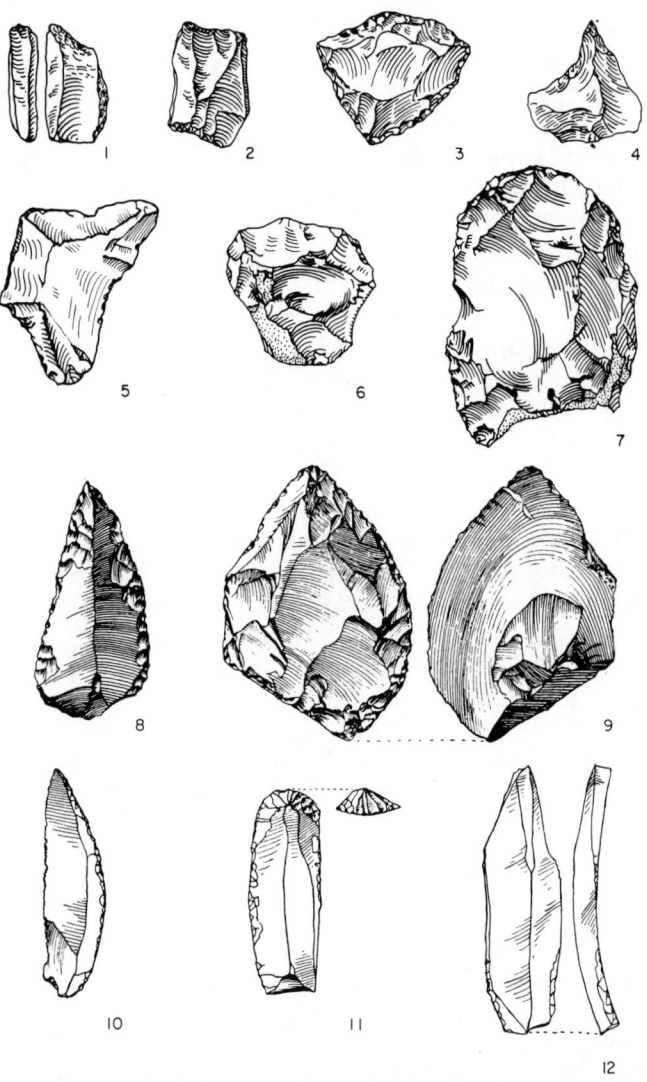

SMALLER STONE TOOLS (approximately one-half natural size)
Very early—Developed Oldowan, made from quartz or quartzite, from top of Bed II Olduvai Gorge, Tanzania, approximately one half million years old (redrawn after Mary Leakey): 1) engraving tool (*burin*); 2) squarish scaled tool (*outil écaillé*); 3) scraper chipped all around; 4) awl.

Explanations of diagrams continued:

ance of modern man. In Australia they may have hung on until 20 thousand years ago, or even later.

During their heyday representatives of this division of men spread to Africa, and on the way either invented in India or picked up from another people the idea of making important types of implements known as hand-axes and cleavers. These were not made, however, like the ones called by the same names in Europe, not made from the inner cores of nodules, but from large flakes or split pebbles, with a characteristic style of flaking. When these people arrived in Africa with their Madrasian-Stellenbosch stone culture (named from the extremes of its distribution), they lived for a time side by side with *Telanthropus* (with some cultural exchange) until the latter, who were smaller and made more delicate Oldowan implements, in a different style, disappeared.

They remained until displaced, in turn, by modern

—Approximately contemporaneous (Cromerian) flints from a filled-in or "fossil" cave exposed in a quarry near Westbury-sub-Mendip, Somerset, England (redrawn after Miss M. O. Miller in article by M. J. Bishop in *Nature* Jan. 10, 1975): 5) flake with single large scar on back side; 6) crude bifacial flint worked from flattened pebble; 7) bifacial scraper chipped all around. Similar artifacts of the same age have been found in the Vallonnet sea-cave in Southern France and in Hungary.

Late (Mousterian)—Flints from Le Moustier rock shelter near Peyzac (Dordogne), France: 8) point; 9) side-scraper (*racloir*).

Very late (upper Paleolithic)—Blade tools: 10) Châtelperron backed-blade knife point, Châtelperron (Allier), France; 11) Aurignacian end-scraper (*grattoir*) Cae Gwyn, Vale of Clwyd, N. Wales; 12) Magdalenian graver (*burin bec-de-flûte*), La Madeleine rock shelter, Tursac (Dordogne), France.

Figs. 1–7 redrawn by Mary Douglass.
Figs. 8–12 after C. O. Waterhouse in *Man the Toolmaker* by Kenneth P. Oakley, with permission of the Trustees of the British Museum (Natural History).

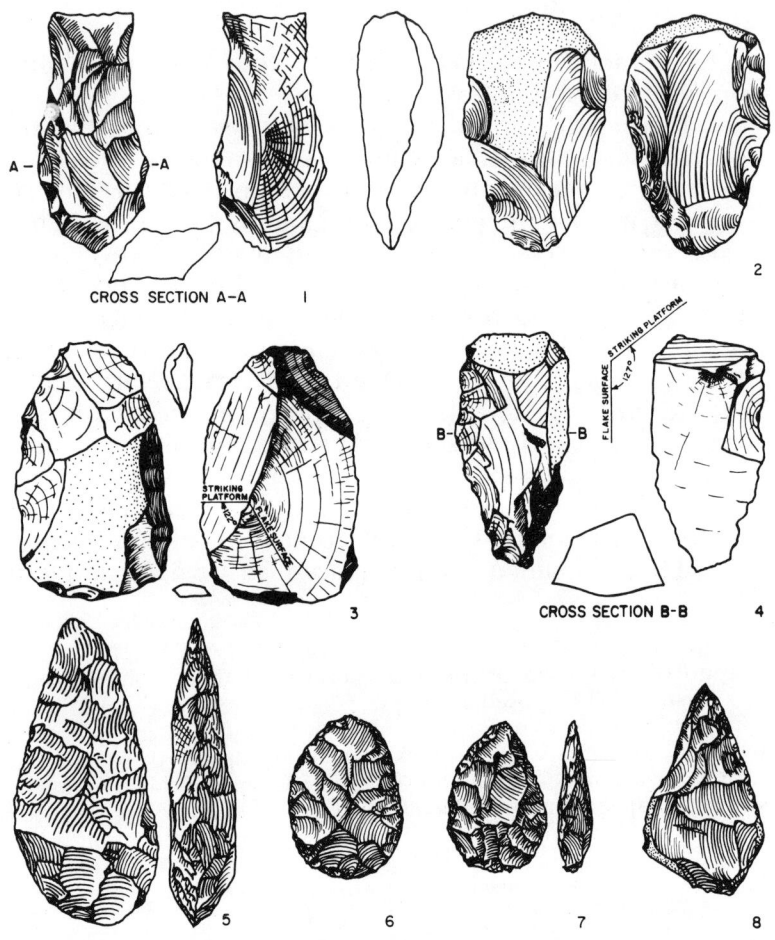

LARGER STONE TOOLS (approximately one fourth natural size or less)

Early—Madrasian implements from India: 1) large cleaver (15.2 cm long) made of dolerite, side-struck as in Vaal technique, from Pravara, Nevassa (after Sankalia); 2) handaxe from Orissa (after Mohapatra).
—Stellenbosch implements from the Vaal River, South Africa: 3) cleaver; 4) end-struck handaxe (after Van Riet Lowe).

Medium age (Acheulian)—5) Lava handaxe from Olorgesailie, Kenya, East Africa; 6) Ovate handaxe from south of Wadi Sidr, Palestine; 7) Ovate handaxe showing edge twist characteristic of middle Acheulian, from the *argile rouge* on the 30-metre terrace of the Somme at St. Acheul, near Amiens, France; 8) Micoquian-type late Acheulian handaxe from the brickearth, Hoxne, Suffolk, England.

All figures redrawn by Mary Douglass. Figs. 5–8 after C. O. Waterhouse in *Man the Toolmaker* by Kenneth P. Oakley, by permission of the Trustees of the British Museum (Natural History).

man with true handaxes and other cultural innovations, but in the extreme south and northwest corners of Africa they lingered on, as in Asia, until almost the end of the ice ages. The latest ones in both regions became more extreme in their physiological contrasts with modern man, before becoming extinct. At one time they even crossed over from the northwest corner of the continent into Spain, and nearby areas of southern France; and earlier another branch, probably from the east, invaded eastern Europe, as represented by the famous Mauer jaw from Heidelberg, Germany.

Very sparsely scattered stone relics indicate the presence of men in very early times in Europe also; but conditions were not so good for the preservation of their bones, or even of recognizable undisturbed assemblages of early artifacts, as they were by the sides of lakes in arid volcanic regions in East Africa, or in the volcanic deposits of southeastern Asia and elsewhere. Not until later uplifts caused rivers to entrench their courses and caves to form along their valley sides and there were younger, still undisturbed land surfaces covered by sediments on river terraces and plains, did the remains of men get preserved so as to become moderately well-represented in the records of Europe. The back part of a skull, indicating a very large brain, discovered in Hungary and associated with characteristic well-formed stone implements of a type first known from Clacton-on-Sea in England, suggest the presence there of a man of advanced type for the time. There are also advanced relics from Israel, though the age there is disputed. A very early skull (recently revised age 1.8 million years) with a large brain for the time and other more modern features, known by its museum number as No. 1470, and a juvenile skull No. 1590 already with a large brain, and modern-type leg bones No. 1481 have been found in East Africa, suggesting the existence even then of a more progressive type of man (because he was so much

PROFILE SKULL OUTLINES OF EARLY TO MODERN MEN
In Order of Age.

1. *Homo*, sp., KNM-ER 1470, from East Rudolf, East Africa.
2. *Australopithecus africanus* (or *Plesianthropus transvaalensis*) from South Africa.
3. *Pithecanthropus erectus* from Java.
4. *Homo sapiens*, early variety, from Skhul Cave, Mt. Carmel, Israel.
5. *Homo neanderthalensis* from La Chapelle, France.
6. *Homo sapiens sapiens* from Cro-Magnon, France.

No. 1 from *Nature*, Vol. 242, April 13, 1973, p. 449; no. 4 after Charles E. Snow in the *Bull. Amer. School of Prehistoric Research*, Vol. 17, 1953. Others from Bernard Campbell, 1966. All figures redrawn by Mary Douglass. The figures give an approximate idea of the relative sizes of brains.

earlier) than the Hungarian and Israeli remains. After the foregoing was written, a still earlier progressive type of man has been discovered in Ethiopia near the Red Sea and another at Laetolil just south of Olduvai. Some or all of these may really belong to the genus *Homo*.

From a much later time (about a quarter-million years ago), the back part of another skull of modern form occurred at Swanscombe, England, associated with a handaxe culture (typical Acheulian) such as prevailed in western Europe for a long time, and appeared in East Africa at the time that more leg bones of modern type appeared at Olduvai and modern skulls with very light brow ridges at Kanjera, overlapping in this region the presence of *Pithecanthropus* and his culture. Another skull, found near Steinheim in southern Germany, but not with Acheulian culture (except for one fair quality handaxe in beds of the same age not far away), having only some of the branch line features (like heavy brow ridges, which suggests the beginning of a branch line), nevertheless gives some indication of progressive characters at that time. From a later, but still early time, men of modern type have been found at Omo in Ethiopia, at Jebel Kafzeh in Israel, at Veternica Cave west of Zagreb, Yugoslavia, and at Fontéchevade in France. Their cultures all belong to the Lower Paleolithic or older part of the Old Stone Age (*paleo*, ancient; and *lith*, stone). Nearly all, or at least most, of these belong to the modern species *Homo sapiens*, and perhaps all to the genus *Homo* in the strict sense (excluding *Pithecanthropus* and *Telanthropus*).

At a remarkably late date a different group of men appeared, known as Neanderthals, who can be seen, both by their anatomical features and by their culture (a part of what is commonly called Mousterian or Middle Paleolithic), to have been derived from the preceding group. Splitting from the same group they show, especially at first, many similar variations; but apparently

PALATAL VIEWS OF HIGHER ANTHROPOIDS

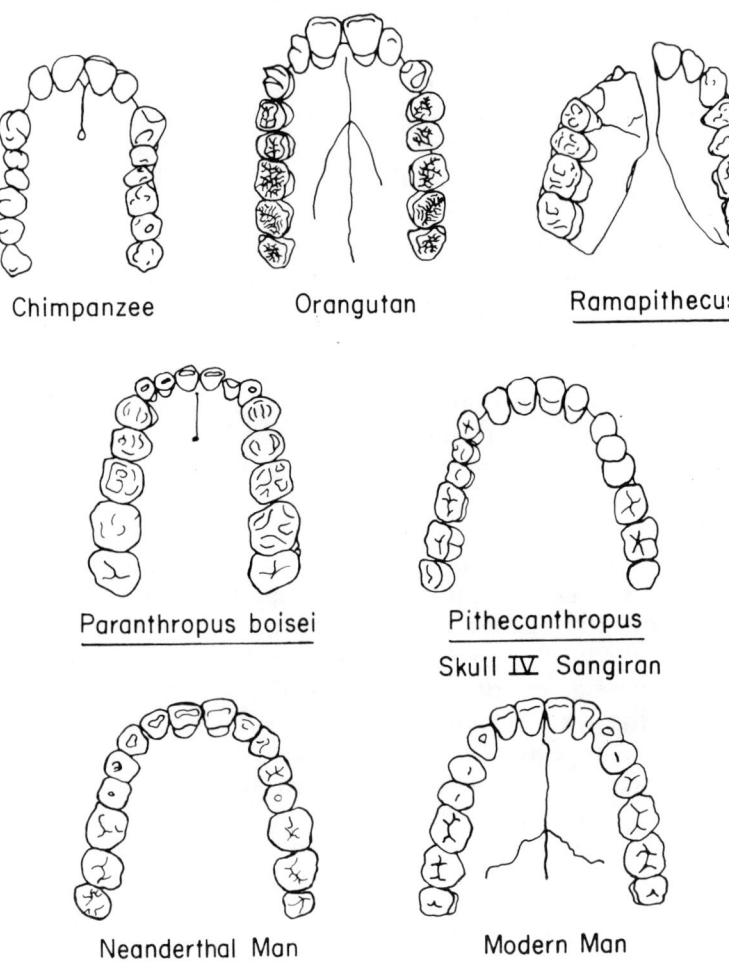

Chimpanzee   Orangutan   <u>Ramapithecus</u>

<u>Paranthropus boisei</u>   Pithecanthropus

Skull IV Sangiran

Neanderthal Man   Modern Man

Le Moustier

Ramapithecus, from the lower Pliocene of the Siwalik Hills in northern India, after Elwyn L. Simons in his "Early Relatives of Man," in the *Scientific American* for July, 1964, copyright © by Scientific American, Inc. All rights reserved.

Paranthropus boisei, from Olduvai Gorge, East Africa, after P. V. Tobias in *Olduvai Gorge* Vol. 2.

Pithecanthropus erectus, variety *robustus,* from Java, after Franz Weidenreich in the *Anthropological Papers of the Amer. Mus. Nat. Hist.,* N.Y., Vol. 40, 1945. (This variety was earlier named *Homo modjokertensis* for a child which, being a child, showed many more features of modern man. The gaps (diastema) between the teeth in this specimen, as in the apes, may be unusual, as other specimens of *Pithecanthropus* do not show them.)

they adopted a way of life somewhat like the ways of the early Asiatics and early Africans, which involved heavy teeth and jaws, the strong pull of jaw and neck muscles, and the squeezing out of heavy brow ridges. Their leg bones were curved and the big hole in the base of the skull (*foramen magnum*) for passage of the spinal chord was rather far to the rear, but it has been argued that these do not indicate a stooped posture. Their lower arm bones were bowed apart as if they had very heavy muscles, and their hand bones had very different proportions from ours. Their skulls were long and low, projecting in front in a slanting face and even more to the rear, flat at the base and bulging at the sides, so that their brains, as big as ours or bigger, were small in the forepart. They had no hollow in the cheek bones below the eyes (*canine fossa*), and their chins were generally receding, without the central groove that separates the two protuberances in our chins. The temporal bone at the side of the skull had features very distinct from ours, and Drs. Philip Lieberman and Edmund S. Crelin have shown, from the angle of the styloid process of the temporal bone and from the angle of the jaw and the flattened base of the skull, that Neanderthal Man had only a limited capability of vocal communication, being physiologically unable to make the long vowel sounds and certain consonants (*k, g,* etc.) of human speech. This may have been the chief reason for his inability to compete with modern man and his relatively sudden extinction within a few thousand years in Europe, though he may have lived on a little longer in northwest Africa. There may have been, of course, numerous other factors

———————

Homo neanderthalensis, from Le Moustier, France, after Wm. K. Gregory and Milo Hellman, also from the *Anthrop. Pap. Amer. Mus. N.H.,* Vol. 28, 1926, pl. 24.

All figures redrawn by Mary Douglass.

contributing to his extinction, and some of them may have been more important.

Typical Neanderthals lived mostly in the mountainous regions of central Europe, including the surrounding foothills and the cavernous sides of river valleys, though at the height of their expansion they may have spread more widely into the lowlands of western Europe. A related division (species or variety) was distributed eastward across the plains of southern Russia to Uzbekistan, and around the eastern end and southern shore of the Mediterranean (across northern Africa). Archaic types of men farther away in China, Java, and southern Africa, attributed to this group because they were contemporaneous, may rather be holdovers of the *Pithecanthropus* group. This Near East and North African division of Neanderthaloids was less extreme in its deviation from progressive human physiologic developments, although its cultures are clearly related to those of the so-called classic Neanderthals of Europe.

In the Near East and North Africa, as well as in western Europe (mostly in maritime areas) there is evidence that more progressive cultures and men preceded the Neanderthals, were contemporaneous with them, and finally expanded to squeeze them out. In Palestine, which has always been the crossroads of the world, as well as in France, the rapid succession of contrasting cultures shows that at least two different groups of men were inhabiting these regions at various times. When populations were sparse, it is likely that the individual bands mostly avoided each other without serious conflict. It would not be surprising if early in the separation of the groups there was some interbreeding when they came into the same region. At Mount Carmel in Israel this may have happened near the middle of the time of overlap, or after, but if so, it seems to have been unusual, for the cultures and groups seem to have kept their distinctiveness fairly consistently. The course of events is complicated, however, by occasional occurrences of the wrong kind of man with a culture, apparently as victims or wanderers, such as were found at Amud in Israel (a somewhat Neanderthaloid with a very early progressive culture) and at Fontéchevade in France preceding the Neanderthals there (modern men with an early backward culture). Yet it is to be expected that the careful gathering of more evidence will make still clearer the preponderance of associations.

Splitting off at such a late date from the main line of progressive human development, it is to be expected that the Neanderthals would show many indications of advanced features. Besides the big brains, there is more evidence of group action, available to us since the chances of preservation were becoming so much better. Hunting of large animals in groups with spears tipped with stone points represents an advance over the *Telanthropus* level of group hunting, where they had to drive the animals into a swamp and kill them with plain wooden spears. Extra attention during the burial of the dead shown by rubbing them with red ochre indicates, at least among those who started the tradition, a caring and regret for the loss, with an attempt to reverse or lessen its impact. Both the caring and the ability to express it had, no doubt, risen far above the level of their beginnings among the Therapsids. Arranging of stones or bones around the body and placing a slab above it to protect it may also be related, or it may indicate merely a precaution to keep scavengers from making unpleasant exposures.

The finding of numerous grains of flower pollen among the graves in Shanidar Cave, Iraq, is suggestive of the early use of flowers to express feeling, but it should be checked to see if the wind blew flower pollen into uninhabited caves or, if not, to see if flower pollen throughout the finer portions of cultural debris would possibly suggest the gathering of flowers merely for pleasure. The finding of the skeleton of a man, also at Shanidar, who had had a birth defect crippling his right arm and shoulder but who had nevertheless been cared for as a child, protected and supported until he reached the age of about forty (very old for those times), provides more tangible evidence of the extent of the development of group cooperation and caring since the beginnings in Therapsid times. But many of the assumptions commonly made about supposed religious activities are probably not justified. They involve too much projections backwards of modern attitudes. The evidence for a so-called "bear cult" has been shown to be very flimsy. Very likely the conscious arrangement of cave bear skulls in several places is related to efforts to capture more bears, like the hunting dances of later times, but that is quite different from worship. The abundant evidence of cannibalism has also been attributed to ritualism, but whether just for food or for power over others, it is hardly religious or progressive. The advanced features of the Neanderthals are most probably derived from their immediate, more progressive ancestors.

The Acheulian handaxe culture of Swanscombe Man evolved gradually and continuously in western Europe, until during the time of the Neanderthals it graded into what has been known by the misleading—as well as cumbersome—name of Mousterian of Acheulian Tradition (MAT); and that in its turn graded into the following Perigordian culture of the modern type of man. It would contribute to a much clearer awareness of relationships (be more apt) to call it the Acheulian-Perigordian Transition (APT). The cultures of Neanderthal men diverged from this until they disappeared. In the Near East and North Africa, besides the Acheulian, a culture known as Pre-Aurignacian or Amudian preceded the Neanderthal cultures, emphasizing the elements already beginning in the Acheulian that became characteristic of the later Aurignacian and other Upper Paleolithic cultures of Europe which, including the Perigordian, are the undisputed products of the modern type of man. Handaxes were gradually replaced by stone knives (backed blades), and other kinds of blades (elongate flakes), end-scrapers, and engraving instruments (burins), most of these struck by using a punch, from a core with a previously prepared flattish striking platform, leaving a central remnant recognizable as a prismatic core. There were also bone implements. In contrast, the Neanderthal cultures emphasized broader flakes knocked probably by a direct blow from shallower discoidal or "tortoise" cores, worked up into side-scrapers and spear points, differing less from the flake parts of the preceding upper Acheulian. They also sometimes struck flakes from prepared striking platforms.

After the abrupt disappearance of the Neanderthals, the modern men of the Upper Paleolithic had anatomical features indistinguishable from the present, beginning about 40,000 years ago. These include chins that are usually projecting, and even if not projecting, are characterized by a central groove (which you can feel in your own chin) with bumps (eminences) on each side of it. This development may be related to the practice of speech, making more space on the inside for working the tongue, and putting the strengthening on the outside. Oddly, the relics of the earliest progressive men do not have the jaws preserved, while the archaic men of northwest Africa and Heidelberg Man are only represented by jaws (with non-progressive chins) and teeth. Perhaps the oldest modern chin known so far is the one from Omo, Ethiopia, contemporary with the early Neanderthaloids. It would be most interesting to know what kinds of chins Swanscombe, Fontéchevade, and Kanjera men had, and whether the capacity for making the sounds of modern speech developed before the

Neanderthaloids split off or among their modern-type contemporaries. It surely didn't develop suddenly after the Neanderthals disappeared. Another feature of the jaws of Upper Paleolithic modern-type men is the strong forward convergence of the rows of side teeth, in contrast to the weak convergence of Neanderthals and other branch line men and to the parallel rows of most other Primates. This seems to have been a regular feature of main line representatives since the end of the Mesozoic, including early tarsier-like ones, with the reduction of canines, suggesting less emphasis on the mouth for primary food-getting and defense, and more use of the hands for such purposes.

The skulls of the known main line representatives of the genus *Homo* rounded up behind in a smooth curve from the centrally placed *foramen magnum* and also arched over the top, with vertical sides, a high forehead, and a more nearly vertical face. The brow ridges, usually light, were characterized as now by a shallow diagonal depression over each eye which, with the central separation, really divides them into four parts. The narrow nose hole and the hollow below each eye (*canine fossa*) are the culmination of the tendency all through the development of the Primates for the reduction of the snout and caving in of the face to make way for the improvement of sight.

The main line men seem to have inhabited the flat plain open-air sites and coastal areas where preservation was less likely, though they were already spread to the far corners of the Old World (western Europe, South Africa, and Borneo); but after the disappearance of the Neanderthals, during the coldest part of the last glaciation, they took more to the caves in Europe, and they and their cultures were more abundantly preserved. Their cultures advanced rapidly from one stage to another. They covered the walls of caves with very high quality realistic engravings and paintings, and they carved bone, stone, and wooden figures. Among the carvings, from the later Perigordian and its central European equivalent on, were female figurines ("venuses") with the feminine parts exaggerated, perhaps used as charms to promote the fertility and well-being of game (and later of crops), and showing appreciation of the role of women in reproduction, and perhaps also vaguely in promoting the unity, prosperity, and well-being of the community through their expressions of affection and their gathering of food, caring for the young, and other services.

One factor that may have had a great influence on increasing the cohesiveness and social cooperation within groups of early men was the greatly heightened sexual sensitiveness of the human female's capacity for deeply satisfying orgasm, which was probably the cause of her extending the period of her receptivity until it became continuous, in contrast to the condition in all other higher Primates and other animals. At present we have no way of deducing when that may have occurred, whether at the time of the splitting of men and higher Primates, or the splitting of *Homo* in the restricted sense from the other early men, or the splitting off of Neanderthals, or even later. We do not know if it could be related to such occurrences as the loss of bodily hair covering or the introduction of frontal contact during intercourse. It has been suggested that the first true speech, consisting of standardized symbolic expression in sound of combined observational content and feeling, may have occurred in connection with the stimulation of such more intimate relations. Though the potentials of affection in personal physical relations have no doubt continued to rise to the present day, it is obvious that in recent millennia their realization by each individual has become more and more severely limited psychologically in nearly all cases, as will be explained later, by increasing self-centeredness, illustrated by drives to exploit, on the part of both men and women.

The Upper Paleolithic cultures, including the figurines, were carried from central Europe northeastward across Siberia, and men crossed the broad land bridge of Beringia (exposed during the times of great cold by the locking up of water in glaciers, thus lowering the sea level), and so entered Alaska and the rest of the Americas. Those who remained in the far north of Siberia during the last cold maximum became adapted to the very severe climatic conditions there and became Mongoloids, afterward spreading southward and occupying all of Asia down to the Himalayas.

As the glaciers melted back and the big game hunters were still pursuing the reindeer and other cold region creatures farther north, forests grew up and took over the former open tundra areas of the mid-latitudes of Europe and elsewhere. Men in the mid-latitudes hunted smaller game, including fish and waterfowl, and (it was probably women mostly) gathered the more abundant vegetable products, as well as shellfish, etc. These were Mesolithic (Middle Stone Age) times. The practice spread of setting small, sharp stone flakes (microliths) in wooden or bone handles (hafting them) for use as implements. In the Near East especially they made sickles with these microliths to harvest wild grains. In various places, from southeast Asia to equatorial Africa, efforts were made to encourage the growth of desirable plants (fruits, tubers, etc.).

Soon after that, culminating in the Near East about 10,000 years ago, came the Neolithic or agricultural revolution, a series of major innovations in rather quick succession: the planting of seeds to raise harvests at a later time, the domestication of animals (dogs and the food animals, sheep, goats, pigs), weaving, pottery, and the grinding of some stone implements to produce shapes more useful than could be had by Paleolithic and Mesolithic chipping alone. These advances greatly increased the food supply, made possible settled farming communities of much larger populations, and caused profound psychological changes and change in art styles, as will be described in the next section. It is probable that women were primarily responsible for the agriculture. It was they who mainly gathered and looked after the wild vegetable provisions. It was they who stayed close to the camp caring for the children, and who saw that some of the grain that had been spilled was sprouting. Some of them must have put two and two together and started purposeful planting, though that would have involved a tremendous enlargement of the time sense— to foresee the harvest in the far-away future. But it was the women who had the fertility power, who could plant a grain and most likely make it grow to fruition. The female figurine charms were still being carried. Very likely women then had a more esteemed place in the most progressive societies than they had ever had before or than they have had since for a long time, if indeed they have, on the average, fully recovered that position yet. But some modern societies are approching greater sensitivity on that subject and on a number of others that may help to give us more balanced development and so lead to greater well-being.

It can be seen that evolution, guided by the nature of reality in life itself and in the environment, has produced a continual, if not quite steady, advance in main line qualities toward what are recognized as the highest human values, toward sensitivity, awareness, and receptivity, attributes that reach their highest expression in genuine human love. Though there may be some inaccuracies in the foregoing summary of the record, the overall trend is clear. (A much more detailed and thorough presentation of this record is now being prepared in a larger volume entitled *The History and Meaning of Life*.) In spite of some temporary setbacks, there has occurred wave after wave of forward advances. Life has attained step by step greater freedom from the limitations of the environment, and at the same time has made greater advances toward genuine love.

That is the way it has to be, for love cannot be genuine without freedom, and freedom cannot be valid without love. But freedom means opportunity to make mistakes, and so we have an explanation of the origin of evil. Throughout the history of life there have always been many more making mistakes than have been on the main line. While making a biologic advance the main line is relatively obscure, and then, when it begins to be successful and spread out, nearly all the radiants begin to specialize and get off the track. ("Many are called but few are chosen." "Wide is the gate, and broad is the way, that leadeth to destruction, and many there be which go in thereat: because narrow is the gate and small is the way which leadeth unto life, and few there be that find it.") This process may seem wasteful, but it is the only way that freedom can be developed, and eventually a higher type of being who will understand and voluntarily choose the right. Presumably we do not yet have full perspective, and if we could see from a higher perspective we might be able to recognize either that the separateness of individuals is not so important as we usually assume, or that the setback to those who in our view persist to the visible end in going the wrong way is somehow only temporary. (It is possible to imagine a way or ways in which one or both could be true, and there may be other ways we cannot imagine.) In any case, the product which the natural system is working to produce is so wonderful, and the process so marvelously adapted to that result, that we can be truly enthusiastic about it and trust it. It requires of us only that we recognize it and voluntarily go along with it. That is one important aspect of the worship of God. It shows God infinitely superior to one that could only produce creatures by special creation, doomed as automatons to play the parts designed for them. It shows an Ultimate Reality favorable to (benevolent toward) the production of what we recognize as the highest human qualities.

Moreover, in our vast universe there are almost certainly billions of other places where conditions have been suitable for the origin and development of life, and where inevitably life has arisen and advanced, in some cases far beyond ours, in some equal to ours, and in some far behind. In all these cases the nature of the surrounding reality surely conditions the development so that, in spite of an infinite variation in accidental shapes and forms, the same fundamental principles of life apply, stressing an all-round balanced development of capacities and increasing sensitivity, awareness, alertness, and receptivity. A little thought will show that no alternative scheme, like stressing the unbalanced, the rigid, the callous, the non-cooperative, would work. Hence it can be seen that even though all life on the earth should be annihilated by nuclear warfare and so end in utter failure here, the success of life-producing reality in many other places, and the success of the whole, would still be assured.

There is very great danger that the worst may happen here in the next few decades: all life be killed off or possibly only a remnant of life be preserved. But such an outcome need not happen, even here. We have enough information and capacity to make a paradise on earth, either for just a few especially receptive individuals in the short time left us, or for a larger number permanently, or perhaps eventually for all. We are living in the most exciting time in the history of the world, with both the dangers and the opportunities greater than ever before. The road is open for any individual who sincerely wishes to seek and find the deep, rich, lasting joy of true happiness now, to find that happiness by helping others do the same, and to help avert the catastrophe for all.

Psychological Evolution, and the
Modern Psychological Problem

The psychological condition of men in the Upper Paleolithic and up to the time of the Neolithic or agricultural revolution can be reconstructed in accordance with several lines of valid scientific observation. The data for these observations include: the minds of still primitive peoples who have changed less than we have since the Upper Paleolithic; the relics left behind by the Upper Paleolithic peoples themselves, especially their art; the early developmental stages of modern infants and toddlers; the deep subconscious of modern adults; and the psychological conditions of other modern Primates, especially the socially less neurotic ones. All of these point in the same direction and give the impression of a state of consciousness characterized by differences from our own that are significant. This has been called by Gerald Heard the "co-conscious stage," and by Fritz Kunkel the Primitive "We." Recognition of the differences from our own shows why many assumptions customarily made, about early peoples acting much as we would act under the conditions they faced, are invalid.

Cave men, and their contemporaries who inhabited open-air sites, normally passed the whole of their rather short lives in small hunting-gathering groups of not more than about twenty to thirty individuals (men, women, and children). As the groups were relatively stable, the members got to know each other very well and acted together in close-feeling relationship. The unity of fellowship was constant and strong to a degree we seldom experience today. Individuals acted mainly in accord with feelings shared by the entire group (they saw things all the same way—collective representations), and they did very little independent thinking, such as we do today, either about themselves or about other things. They were held together, no doubt, by deep affection, which was so universal that they were not conscious of it. Indeed, they were hardly self-conscious at all. Any tendency to deviate from the customs of the group would have been considered so peculiar that it would immediately have been rejected by the group with disgust and the individual excluded, which would have been such a severe deprivation emotionally as well as physically (probably fatal) that everyone intuitively avoided it. That made for stability, of course, but it kept originality to a minimum, and it accounts for the slow rate of progress (very slow by our standards, though fast compared with earlier times).

The group not only felt a strong unity among themselves, but they also felt a unity with most of nature (had many variations of what have been called "mystical participations"), though they would operate as a unit against predators and evil influences, and would drive out groups of men—not known to be friendly—who invaded their territory. Since there was room, such groups normally avoided each other, and the outsiders would normally withdraw from the territory of a local group without a fight. Death did not seem of great moment, for it did not exclude the person from the fellowship, as he would reappear in dreams; and in accordance with their assumption of what we have called reincarnation, he would come back to them as a newborn infant. They apparently expected the animals to feel the same way, for their dances in preparation for hunting were often directed toward persuading the animals to come into the neighborhood and be killed, and afterward they would try to make amends to the continuing unseen reality of the one they had killed so he wouldn't feel badly about it and influence others of his kind against being caught. They clearly had no conscious beliefs, such as we have, but regarded the seen and the unseen influences as equally real. There were no specific gods, but a sense of all-pervading power such as some later peoples have called *mana*. In spite of very serious hardships, it is probable that the level of real happiness was high. Modern primitives have been pushed out to the undesirable left-over places of the world, where the environments are so harsh that they can barely get along. Hence they are very inferior representatives of what the early main line groups were like in the most stimulating and favorable places. Most of these points and many others have been brought out very effectively by the French anthropologist Lévy-Bruhl, who quotes instance after instance from reported observations of modern primitives. He has been criticized most severely for his intellectual presentations, but the essence of his work has to be absorbed feelingly between the lines.

The very realistic art of the Upper Paleolithic is part of the indication of specific objectivity and close-feeling attitudes of the artists, who felt they were reaching the animals through mystical participation between the animals and the pictures. They were not trying to impress other men of their group, with whom they already had close fellowship. The specific objectivity shows that they were not attempting to generalize into classifications but were absorbed with the individual, having what Martin Buber would call an "I-Thou" attitude toward the animals, which gave them the power of graphic recollection, otherwise known as eidetic imagery, such as is shown by some young children and primitive people today. Also they saw the creature as a whole, not analyzing it, not mentally trying to take it apart. It is not possible to classify without analyzing, without picking out some part or parts common to all items in the class. Hence they thought little in terms of classes of objects. Later forms of Mesolithic and Neolithic art become diagrammatic, showing the introduction of analysis and classification.

Very young modern infants have a close-feeling relationship with the mother that amounts practically to oblivion for everything else, almost as much on the part of the mother as for the child when she is with the child. Kunkel calls this the original "We." Feeling predominates, not thinking. Moreover, the subconscious of the modern adult consists largely of powerful feeling elements which mainly determine important personal decisions, though the conscious faculties will usually rationalize afterward to produce thinking explanations. The conscious mental functions are an historically later development, and they have pushed the feeling part down into the subconscious. This suppression has also tended to make many of the feelings negative. Primitive peoples are very much aware of the evil effects of negative feelings, and they make strenuous efforts to prevent the negative feelings from arising and to allay their effects if they do. In this, we can learn something from them.

Modern Primates other than man show many forms of group actions, and although most of them show signs of being specialized and degenerate, we can get some clues from them. Howler monkeys, for instance, show more equalitarian behavior than those groups with self-conscious dominant males. Yet even baboons and gorillas, as well as chimpanzees, show much positive group and personal feeling. There must have been similar diversity among men also, but it is to be presumed that the most successful main line groups were so because of strong coherence, with just enough balancing tolerance for diversity to allow for some progress.

The beginnings of the most primitive or elementary religion can be discerned in the Upper Paleolithic. Close fellowship in the group was everything to its members. The relation of each member to all the members (to what we call abstractly "society as a whole") was more important than to any one particular member. If one was lost, there were still the others. This basic fact, as explained by Emile Durkheim, began to be symbolized by the *totem*, usually a kind of animal, sometimes a plant, or more rarely an inanimate object such as clouds, wind, moon, water, the summer, fire, smoke, etc., with which all the members of the clan collectively identified themselves. How each clan began to feel itself particularly related to and represented by one particular totem, different from the totem of any other clan they knew about, is not clear. They certainly did not consciously choose a totem as modern groups choose a mascot. But either the tendency was so fundamental that many peoples throughout the world independently adopted some form of it, or it spread from one or more centers, for it is found preserved among primitive peoples from the Australian aborigines to the African bushmen, to the native tribes in the jungles of Brazil, and it must have formerly occupied the areas in between, where later developments have superseded it and so have made its former presence not directly recognizable.

Since the totem symbolized all that was of really great importance to them, it became sacred. Later an object marked with a symbol of the totem became even more sacred. The Australians used (and still use) pieces of wood or polished stone so marked, generally oblong or oval, called *churinga*. Some have been pierced near one end, and a cord of hair through the hole enables them to be whirled rapidly, making a humming noise, as is done in important ceremonies. These are *bull-roarers*. In other places leather thongs are used. The Tasmanians and also the Azilians of south-western Europe had pebbles with symbols painted on them, which must have had similar significance. These are perhaps the earliest examples of symbol writing, with the exception of the Upper Paleolithic tally marks used in southwestern Europe to count time and keep track of the phases of the moon. It is not surprising, in view of the importance of group relatedness, that the Australians have evolved the most intricate and highly developed kinship or human relations system known, based not so much on heredity as on associations, just as we, putting our emphasis in material goods, have developed the most highly integrated technology, and as similarly our ancestors emphasized political organization. The Australians have no chiefs or officers, but they recognize persons with particular talents and are guided by them, without formal government.

Elsewhere, with the Neolithic or agricultural revolution, the rate of change accelerated, and it has continued to speed up more and more ever since. The food supply, greatly enlarged and made more dependable all year round, resulted in a population growth to several hundred in settled farming communities. It was no longer possible to know everyone intimately. The larger community tended to subdivide into smaller units, usually consisting of more or less enlarged families; and then the loyalties of the individual were sometimes divided. Sometimes the interests of one small unit were in conflict with those of other small units or of the community as a whole. To which should the individual be loyal? He had to begin to think for himself as he had not been doing before to any considerable extent. He became aware of his own interests as an individual, and began to become self-conscious. Thus occurred what is known in religious circles as "Original Sin," the origin and essence of all sin: the sense of separation from one's fellows, the idea that you can further your own interests at the expense of others, opening the way to exploitation of others. Thus man "fell" from the close fellowship in the universal Garden of Eden to a knowledge of what is good and what is evil in his own eyes, as he began to till the ground. This sense of separateness was sin, because it began to interfere with progress toward the capacity for highest sensitivity and receptivity, for genuine love, which, as we can see by projecting the trend, is the most advanced foreseeable goal of evolutionary development. He began to feel separate from nature also.

Of course, when man began to think of himself as an individual, he began to realize how small and weak he was, among so many other people and creatures and mighty physical forces, and he began to feel the need for outside help. This marks the change from primitive or elementary religion to what Robert Bellah calls "archaic" religion, accompanied by what is probably the true beginning of magic. Religion was still a communal phenomenon, shared by many (the whole community or the church), with priests or priest-kings deriving their authority from the group, and trying to express by their symbols the nature of reality (the seen and the unseen not distinguished), and to get good results by conforming to it and by supplication or entreaty for the aid of higher powers. The feeling for unity within the group and for relatedness to nature was still the basis of sacredness for their symbols, but the beginnings of self-consciousness are shown in the higher powers (persons, animals, elements of nature, or objects) representing symbolically the product of waking and dreaming personal experiences amalgamated and passed on in feelings and traditions from generation to generation, until they came to be thought of as causing or influencing the experiences they represent.

Magic, on the other hand, was practiced by individuals or small groups more self-consciously, attempting to force undesirable influences to subside or to make any powerful influences do what was desired, outwitting them with formulas that were in themselves meaningless or based merely on analogy with reality. The Australians have changed very slowly compared to other groups and still use less of magic of this kind, but their growing self-consciousness shows in the personal resentments and violence that arise in connection with the only inequalities that have developed in their system—subordinating women to men, and younger men to the middle-aged and older men who have been initiated to full manhood and participation in the councils. The myths about the sacred higher powers were always being modified (as they still are) and they no doubt changed considerably toward their present-day form during this period. Magic and science (as opposed to the practical arts of everyday living) are allied psychologically, since they are both developed as a product of individual self-interest rather than through community feeling. They split when men began to make a distinction between the natural and the supernatural.

Even in agricultural communities the change began gradually at first. Men became only a little self-conscious, and at first only a few of them. For a long time the first individuals who began to think for themselves and be different were put to death, usually feeling and confessing their guilt in the sin of disloyalty to the group, which had caused them to be influences too dangerous to have around. Their execution was not for punishment but for the protection of the fellowship. But when during the Neolithic revolution more and more of them appeared, some sought to protect themselves, and the clever ones became the early magicians and were tolerated because they succeeded in showing the group that they could do something for their benefit (or for their harm if antagonized). But many of them were feared and hated and often eventually eliminated.

However, some groups must have been fortunate enough to be able to look up to a more positive figure, an old wise man or an old wise woman, whom fortune or the greater soundness of their own natures had granted much longer lives than their fellows, accumulating wisdom from experience and sometimes loving respect because of recognized greater innate capacity and even goodness. Such figures are standard symbols, called archetypes, in the dreams of modern adults. Then, also, there must have been some persons with less physical prowess than usual, or some definite handicap, who were not always stupidly downgraded but were instead protected and allowed to work on implements or tend the fires, who became more reflective and were able to communicate new insight to the group. The Neanderthal cripple of Shanidar Cave may have been a very early example. To these or to the older people may be attributed the evolutionary development of religious feelings and attitudes. Finally, also, there must have been unusually dynamic leaders who could evoke more than usual respect, and so influence the group to accept such innovations as they were able to imagine and regard as desirable. And there must have been combinations of each of these types with magicians, uniting magic, religion, and community service, as in modern shamen, who have been held in varying degrees of esteem.

The majority of people were still not far from being co-conscious, and feminine influences still prevailed to hold the group in the unity of close fellowship. The first figures that should be classified as gods were feminine, such as the moon and the sacred cow. Female figurines were still being carried. With the enlarged time-sense they had developed, they would foresee the coming of the next full moon and assemble for moon dances. Probably for a long time this was done purely for the joy of experiencing, in the rhythm of the dance, the temporarily restored feeling of close fellowship which they sensed was slipping from them. The more self-conscious the individuals became, the more they became consciously aware of their dependence on the group, and the more they may have taken satisfaction in religious ritual for this reason also, as pointed out by Durkheim. Only later would some more self-conscious individuals, such as the magicians, begin to wonder what they did it for, and rationalize it as a rite to promote the fertility of the game in the forest, the crops in the field, the domestic animals, and even the human population. It undoubtedly did contribute to the last.

Many of these changes may have begun somewhat before the Neolithic revolution, but they were so greatly speeded up by it that it is legitimate to think of them as mainly occurring then. An Upper Paleolithic dancer, dressed in an animal skin, has been called a magician or sorcerer, though he was not necessarily such. The drawings and paintings of animals in caves may have been fundamentally to bring about closer feeling relations with the animals so that they would willingly cooperate in being caught. There must have been great diversity in the stage of development of different groups, until the innovations of the Neolithic revolution forced many of them in a particular region to go through stages relatively rapidly and nearly simultaneously. The revolution spread rather slowly from its origin in the Near East, not arriving in northern Europe until a few thousand years later, and arising probably independently in some other areas such as southeast Asia, Central and Andean America, and perhaps some place or places in Africa, though the last likely spread from the Near East, too. The latest studies seem to show that some innovations started earlier in Central Europe. Present evidence indicates that sheep were domesticated about 9000 B.C., goats about 7500 B.C., and cattle about 6500 B.C.

It is even possible that some kind of degenerative

psychological change had taken place much earlier among the Neanderthals, as indicated by their cannibalism, whether the latter was purely for food or was ritualistic, for power. Such may have been a more important cause of their extinction than their deficiency of speech or of ecologic adaptation. The *Pithecanthropus* groups of the Far East (notably at Peking and Solo) also show clear evidence of cannibalism, signifying self-destructive currents within the population. By the time the most progressive *Homo sapiens* peoples encountered the disruptive effects of the Neolithic revolution, they had already produced enough creative, positive advances to counteract the negative effects; but the positive and negative kinds of developments have continued to struggle with each other ever since, and more recently the Industrial Revolution has introduced so many more technological advances in such a short time that there is a real question whether we can now overcome and survive the further effects of psychological deterioration, involving extreme individual isolation, with increasing negative feelings and intensifying conflicts.

In the course of time, after the Neolithic revolution, some of the families (or just the menfolk with them), taking care of domestic animals (sheep, goats, or cattle), found that they had to drive their herds farther and farther out to reach good pastures, and eventually they drifted into the habit of staying out with the animals and became nomads. In the rougher conditions of nomadic life, with a preponderance of men, they adopted a more masculine orientation, glorying in their greater strength, and worshiping the sun and the sacred bull. At first the nomadic groups may have been only subcultures, returning periodically to the settlements and being welcomed; but some stayed out so long as to become alienated, and then they could only return to their former farming group, or some other, by the use of force. If they forced their way in, they would become the dominant group, but in time they would be absorbed by the larger farming population. The cultures would merge, but they would occupy the prominent places, such as that of the priest-king, a position which had evolved out of the earlier magicians and chieftains into a not-yet-differentiated authority combining policy-making and religious observances. The female figurines disappeared and masculine symbols took their places.

In some regions, just before the introduction of writing and the use of metals for weapons (first copper, then bronze), which were to mark the beginning of civilization, there was a further stage known as the Heroic Age, including the time of Homer, when bands of men loyal to their hero leaders would roam around in search of adventure and the temporary acquisition of women and goods. Since now loyalty was no longer universal, or nearly so, as it had been in Upper Paleolithic times, it became a virtue, and the members of these bands could boast of high sentiments of group loyalty.

The coming of civilization brought the outbreak of violence on a large scale. Groups possessing metallic weapons had such an advantage over all others that they could subjugate wider territories, found empires, and enslave masses of common people. The only evidence of earlier large-scale violence, or war, comes from Stone Age peoples in the region of the middle Nile, where the drying up of the desert forced groups representative of a number of different cultures to crowd closely into a limited area. That may have influenced the direction taken later by the Near East empires. During the empire stage the power of the ruling groups enabled them to be very despotic and cruel. Nevertheless, the successful empires, the ones that lasted longest, were the ones that encouraged religious activities and allowed religious tolerance, for that supplied the increasing numbers of more self-conscious individuals opportunities to exercise their capacities by running the religious establishments or seeking their own salvation. Those are the ones who would have been potential leaders for disrupting the state. The Greek city-states did many of the same things as the Middle East empires, but on a smaller scale, and, there being many of them, they offered diversity, and in some cases, as at Athens, opportunities for better developments. In Africa and other parts of the world the tribes remained mostly at levels of less intensified individualization, except perhaps at Zimbabwe and Middle America, and a few other places.

During and after the Neolithic revolution, as men were becoming more and more self-conscious, and thus self-centered or *egocentric,* there began to be more emphasis on personal property, the degree and timing varying, of course, from region to region and from tribe to tribe. It is likely that formerly men and women considered as their own only a few articles of personal clothing and ornaments, plus tools used in their work, such as weapons for hunting, gathering and culinary implements, jars, bowls, etc. Territorial occupancy and sacred objects had been shared by the group as a whole. Women may have been regarded mainly as cooperating companions or partners, and sexual relations may not have been strictly limited or repressed, but may have been somewhat as in chimpanzee communities. However, with the development of permanent settlements and of agriculture, huts or dwelling units and sometimes pieces of farming land began to be held as the private property of individuals or of biologic families. Women also became the private property of particular individuals, valued probably more for their work than for their sexual attractiveness. Nevertheless their husbands or owners undoubtedly tended, as they became more egocentric, to restrict the sexual expressions of their women to themselves. Even among peoples who are still in a food-gathering stage, like the Australians, egocentricity, social inequality, and possessiveness of women have developed to some extent. Much more among pastoral tribes did the sense of property increase, and wealth was counted in terms of land, livestock, and women, before metals became important.

At least by the time that metals became important in the empire stage and power became concentrated, those who were able to sought to interfere with the natural expressions of affection between the sexes, in order to reserve more privileges for their own group and thereby for themselves. Kings, emperors, nobles, and priests took advantage of their opportunities to engage in licentious orgies, and allowed ordinary men only limited access to the young women who had been taken as temple prostitutes. These sexual excesses naturally produced a reaction, especially among those who were left out and among the families, lovers, and husbands of the girls who were taken. Spokesmen for these groups, prophets, and others, played into the hands of the rulers and licentiates by declaring all sexual contacts bad and developing cults of ascetics, one extreme tending to justify the other and divert attention from the real values of sex. Both aberrations contributed further toward isolating the individual from meaningful human relatedness. Since profligates tend to dissipate all kinds of resources and eventually weaken themselves, while ascetics concentrate energy and resources, the latter were able, when opportunities arose, to overthrow the former privileged groups, and they have maintained a shaky and sometimes only nominal control most of the time since.

As men became more and more individualized, their concepts of gods tended to reduce also to one single individual, though the needs for a variety of aids have caused them to maintain a group of subordinate entities: aspects of God, lesser gods, saints, devils, angels. The diversity of concepts of the nature of Ultimate Reality still continues today.

So many of the individualized men of the ancient

world were killed off in conflicts that in Europe, during medieval times, the main part of the populace subsided into a peasantry not far removed from a co-conscious condition, while the few individualized persons maintained themselves as feudal lords or sought their own individual salvation in monasteries. When the medieval political adjustment began to break up during the Renaissance, with the budding out of more individuals able to think for themselves, able to revive and apply the knowledge attained in ancient times, and to go on from there, there followed in quick succession a series of revolutions in art, in religion, in politics, in economics, and in science. So we have arrived at a stage of extreme individualism that can be best understood as the capitalist-democracy-scientific stage. All these modern expressions of our present psychological condition are related. Without a large measure of economic freedom political freedom cannot last, and vice versa. Science flourishes best with both. The marvelous outward developments and opportunities of the modern world, as well as its evils, are largely due to them. These are spreading all over the world.

But this very rapid progress, still accelerating, has come with a cost so high that we may not be able to pay for it, recover, and survive. The intensity of conflicts is rising at all levels: international wars, economic conflicts within the nations, delinquency and crime, unhappiness in the home, even some types of insanity, in which individuals cannot get along with themselves; racial antagonisms, generation gaps, and ideological gaps between science and religion and between liberals and conservatives in religion, politics, and economics. We have been increasing our thinking, scheming, competitive, egocentric capacities, but we have not kept pace with these by developing our sense of values, our ability to get along with each other, our positive feeling capacities (appreciation, sympathy, kindliness, affection, and genuine love, in contrast to the many things generally called love in our society). Consequently *we do not have a psychological all-round balance.*

We have been violating, extremely seriously, the basic principles of survival that have prevailed during the 600 million years of evolutionary development that we can see clearly. We do not realize that even the majority of us who are not locked up in institutions are so psychologically unbalanced as to be dangerous, threatening our own survival, dissatisfied because we have not found the real satisfactions that produce genuine happiness in life, blaming others for our lack, and so starting or intensifying conflicts. We are negatively sensitive to infringements of our "rights" and to any challenges to our egocentricity, but we are not positively sensitive to the truly great realities in other persons nor to the elements of validity in positions opposing ours.

We lack receptivity to others and a capacity for genuine love because of this egocentricity, which shuts us in like the shell of a mollusk. That is why the psychologists call it the "egocentric shell." Since it is the egocentricity in us that is blocking evolutionary progress toward the greater sensitivity and receptivity of genuine love and giving us a sense of separateness from each other, we can arrive at a more basic definition of sin as egocentricity, and recognize the truth in the Fundamentalist Protestant confession that all of us in modern society are "miserable sinners," varying only from a relatively moderate degree to a greater degree. Since practically everyone brought up in our society is strongly egocentric, and most of us are blind to the form it takes in ourselves, we must be receptive to help from close friends or professionals, who usually can see, even with the perspective of just a simple description, what we cannot see at all. Characteristically, if a person says about some constructive suggestion: "That is the one thing

I will not do," or if he says: "I will tell you at the outset, or once and for all, my problem is not of that nature," it is a good indication that it is close to his blind spot. There is nothing mysterious about this being so, for the vigorous rejection of the important element is the reason why it is most deficient. No one should claim to be exempt from this.

It is egocentricity itself, and not the various patterns in which it comes, that counts; but it helps to understand the patterns and what they do to us so that we may recognize them, no longer be fooled by them, and take strenuous measures to free ourselves. Egocentricity is always self-limiting to the individual, cutting down on creative capacities and on the enjoyment of life, blocking genuine love. Thus, instead of referring to egocentric patterns, it is better to call them self-limiting patterns, to keep reminding ourselves of what they do to us and to be aware that it is very much to our interest to get rid of them as soon as possible.

Fritz Kunkel has described the common egocentric or self-limiting patterns simply and clearly in a little book called *How Character Develops,* which he wrote in English, assisted by Roy E. Dickerson. Everyone tends to follow each of these patterns at one time or another, under varying circumstances, but the one or ones which predominate in a particular individual depend on the relation of that individual to his early childhood environment.

If the parents, or those who perform the functions of parents, are harsh, domineering, and unfeeling, but the child eventually becomes strong enough to outwit or otherwise overcome them, he will tend to be a *nero* (named after the Roman Emperor Nero), seeking to control others by getting power over them: by making a lot of money, by becoming a political, military, economic, or ecclesiastical boss, or by marrying or seducing women who will submit to him (or a woman may do it to a man). But if, on the other hand, the child does not have strength enough to assert himself, he becomes what Kunkel originally called a *gaby* and later termed more expressively a *turtle,* withdrawing within himself and consoling himself in a dream world, while the real world becomes more and more unfavorable around him.

Contrariwise, if the early environment is benevolent and sentimental and the child is relatively weak, he will tend to become a *clinging vine,* monopolizing attention, appealing to sympathy, always needing extra help, over-emphasizing hurts and hardships, and as a consequence—in extreme cases—becoming a chronic invalid. People get tired of being sympathetic, especially when it becomes clear that the person does not do what he can to help himself, or when he is fickle ốr arrogant in overemphasizing the importance of his own tastes, and then it becomes necessary—in order to revive sympathy—to have the need or hardship or incapacity grow worse. The worsening usually develops in the individual as a natural consequence of his previous attitudes. If, however, in such a seemingly benevolent childhood environment the child grows stronger than the environment, he tends to become a *star*, performing before the circle of his admiring relatives, later on in a few cases becoming a movie or television star, but much more often striving to distinguish himself and gain admiration scholastically, athletically, sexually, politically, economically, artistically, or religiously, and so he tries to become a great artist, musician, "lover," writer, businessman, scientist, popular leader, philosopher, etc.

It should be noticed that all of these patterns are life strategies, or ways of trying to gain close fellowship or genuine love by illegitimate methods: the nero by forcing people to act as if they wanted fellowship with him; the star hoping to draw people into close fellowship through admiration; the clinging vine through sympathy; and the turtle living in imaginary fellowships.

Those who do not carry out the aims of their pattern very well think that they could be happy if only they could do it more successfully, but those who reach the pinnacle of success, especially the nero and the star, often begin to suspect, at first rather vaguely, but sometimes later coming to realize acutely that true fellowship and love cannot be found in those ways. This sometimes explains why millionaires, dictators, and the most popular dramatic stars, with what appears everything they could want, may go to the extreme of committing suicide. Clinging vines and turtles often imagine that they could be happy if they could become successful neroes or stars.

But there are other false methods of trying to obtain fellowship and love. Alcohol may create an illusory sense of fellowship, or, for the solitary individual, may take him along the route of the turtle. Drugs promise similar compensations but produce even worse results. The indulgence of lust by the abuse of sex gives a sense of close fellowship briefly or sometimes longer, but unless other factors are involved, sooner or later ends in boredom. Prolonging the day far into the night with trivialities at the expense of sleep, with reduction of thinking and positive feeling capacities, is another form of turtle-like escapism. Such escape from reality often takes the form, then or at other times, of excessive passive amusements, like watching television, reading insubstantial books or papers, or merely indulging in gossiping or other light talk. Gambling and indeed most adventures and other forms of excitement, and sometimes intense concentration on work or even philanthropy, may be other ways of avoiding broader deep thinking and facing an all-round balanced reality. Smoking and overeating, or indulging in the wrong kinds of food, plus the many other forms of self-indulgence, especially those mentioned above, are consolations confessing the individual's failure to find what really counts in life. All of these lead away from, not toward, genuine love and fellowship and progress along the main line.

These egocentric or self-limiting types often make false shows of being helpful. The star is willing to promote his own glory by catering to the immediate desires of a victim even at the expense of that one's long-run welfare, while he is dreadfully afraid to come out into the open with the corrections the other one most seriously needs, for fear of falling to the depths of disfavor. This includes "spoiling" a child, coddling him when it would be better for him to make a larger amount of constructive contribution for himself and for others instead of having so much done for him, often marked by endless repeating of already well-known instructions, and also by not making plain the value of saving the parents' time, efforts, and resources by taking better care of his own clothes, picking up his room, cleaning up his own play messes, etc. The clinging vine clings, not really to help but to retain his grip. This may show up in detail when the vine is excessively affectionate and the victim complains that the clinging makes him (or her) too hot or uncomfortable, and the vine wants to keep on, ceasing only reluctantly; or when the vine is so solicitous or affectionate for a sick person that he interferes with that one's welfare, as when that one needs to rest or sleep. (He puts himself in the way as a cat sometimes does, even tripping a person up, in order to call attention to himself.)

It is more obvious that the nero is using or exploiting his victims (though the others may be doing it just as much). He may promote the welfare of his victims, as a crafty slave-holder may take good care of his slaves to get more service out of them. He may even allow them liberties, if he is assured it will not jeopardize his possessiveness or if he feels he must run that risk in order to preserve his possessiveness, or even merely to take pride in being a "good fellow." The gaby or turtle is least effective in this respect, for he is obviously not contributing to his associates' welfare. He is a burden to them, requiring services, even though he does not dare demand subservience as the nero does, or tries to do. The sex exploiter often poses as a benefactor, and the alcoholic and drug user are most desirous of sharing with others the "good" things they have found. The smoker, the glutton, the gambler, the adventurer, the gossip, and the other forms of escapees all would do the same.

Two or more individuals with interlocking egocentric self-limiting patterns may develop relationships that, for a time, superficially resemble genuine love so closely that only those who have experienced the real thing can recognize the unsoundness in them, until they begin to degenerate, as they are bound to do sooner or later, unless interrupted by something else beforehand that obscures the significance of the final outcome. Neroes naturally prey upon clinging vines and turtles. Clinging vines respond enthusiastically, hoping for a stalwart to climb on, and turtles comply, both kinds often enduring very severe abuse before giving up. Neroes have a harder time with stars, but may captivate them with flattery and hold them for a while until the stars begin to assert themselves. Stars are elated by the adulation of clinging vines, especially within the family, and the vines enthusiastically absorb all the time and energy they can from the stars. But it is an unusual star who is not soon drained dry, especially if there are a number of vines, and does not thereafter become wary of them. In the case of a mother and a single child, the relationship may be prolonged into later life in what Kunkel calls the embalmed "We," a condition that is evident to onlookers as a very sad case.

The star may also seek to shine on turtles and glory in their opening out, sometimes bringing them up to the point where they become partly neroes. But the star seeks many admirers, and if there are many, they cannot be too close. All of these interlocking relationships depend upon each participant exploiting the others for the purposes of his pattern, doing them good only when it coincides with those purposes, but ultimately doing harm by reinforcing their patterns along with his own. In fact, modern society worldwide is characterized, more than by anything else, by being a gigantic system of interlocking egocentricities. On the social scale, above the personal level, advertisers and politicians, and indeed many kinds of business and even religious and other groups, are conspicuous in being out to exploit whomever they can (although they also have constructive functions). It is such a nearly universal practice, and it is so generally taken for granted in television shows and other forms of communication, that it is almost impossible, especially for children, not to be hypnotized into assuming that it must be so.

There are some special varieties of the star pattern that deserve particular attention. Some religious stars try to excel all others by being more humble or pious, and their egocentricity or self-limitation consists largely of spiritual pride. Negative pacifists are ones who do little work directly to establish in the world and in themselves the conditions necessary for peace but rather emphasize, and sometimes with violent antagonism, how bad the militarists are, who are, after all, trying in their way, even though it may be mistaken, to establish peace. Some of these negative pacifists may even be neroes. Service stars are ones who strive to induce people to like them by being "good" to them, often doing many thoughtful kindnesses and continuing services (household, sexual, entertaining, philanthropic, etc.). Usually they run out of energy or other resources, for service stardom requires large quantities, and then they begin to become disillusioned and their egocentricity begins to show through; but a very small proportion endowed with exceptionally rich stores of energy may appear so agreeable, and so much like persons motivated mainly by genuine love, that they are very difficult to distinguish. The main difference is that in order to induce people to like them (or to avoid risking their disliking them) they cater to their egocentricities, their possessiveness, jealousies, limited outlook and aims, reluctance to help themselves, or just plain indolence, and other weaknesses, giving what is wanted even though it is not good for the recipients, in order to be adjudged generous or "nice," and avoiding attempts to exert a strong influence in constructive directions where it might cause offense. This avoidance is often excused by saying that it is necessary to avoid the opposite egocentric extreme of being dictatorial or superior or nagging; but there is a right middle ground that does not involve abdication of responsibility for a large measure of constructive effort, even when and where it is resisted. It seems that these service stars need only change their motivation a little in order to become *good for,* instead of merely *good to,* those around them. They may be the closest to taking the next step forward along the main line of progress that would enable them to share in a rapidly growing, instead of a diminishing creativity and happiness. It would involve the least change in their habits; but persons with all the other patterns may also, like them, take the needed step forward by wearing away great openings in their shells.

A number of experienced persons working on these problems have pointed out that most people are not individuals unified within themselves, but are really a group of personalities operating differently under different circumstances or in different moods. Thomas Kelley speaks of the "Committee of the Selves" in which decisions are made by majority rule or at the insistence of some domineering member, leaving a more or less disgruntled minority. Much internal friction and loss of energy is the result, and of course in cases of very antagonistically split personalities, the disastrous effects are well known. Usually the different selves, or "I's," as they are sometimes called, are not so antagonistic toward each other, and there are many of them, more or less insulated from each other by "buffers," so that often one may act for the whole without being aware of the others. In some cases a number of these selves may become organized to a greater degree into a "center of gravity" that is more representative of the whole. There will then be less friction, and the individual will be more successful with his chosen life strategy. Unfortunately, this center of gravity is usually in one or more of the self-limiting patterns. But in every person there is a self, or "I," that has the potential for developing the capacity for genuine love, even though it is usually suppressed by the egocentric majority, whether organized or not. The problem is how to develop the suppressed "I" so that it can become the center of gravity, with all constructive elements organized around it.

Apparently some work must be done toward eliminating the shell first, or opening wide holes in it, after which the person may become sufficiently receptive to begin to develop the capacity for genuine love. The shell may be gotten rid of in two ways. One is by slowly and persistently wearing it thin through getting an understanding of one's own particular pattern or combination of patterns and opposing it. Some advisors recommend concentrated efforts at first to overcome minor "hang-ups" in order to develop sufficient moral strength to attack the major problem. Meditation, recognized by experts as the elementary level of real prayer, is a powerful method (if properly practiced) of relaxing one's own prejudices, enabling one, among other goals, to see through the distortions of his own pattern and face reality more squarely. The other way is by undergoing a crisis, in which one's life strategy collapses and it becomes obviously hopeless to try to carry it out successfully. This cracks the shell, but the experience is usually very painful, and there is no assurance that a new shell won't form with or without the broken pieces, which may be just as bad or worse than the old one. Occasionally it may produce a new freedom. Kunkel went through such a crisis successfully when, as a highly skilled army surgeon during the First World War, his right arm was blown off. That can occasionally lead to the development of a mature "we." If through a crack or a window worn through a thin place in the shell the real person inside, the suppressed "I," can become receptive to an experience of genuine love, it can be counted on that the accompanying clarity of understanding and joy will eventually melt away the rest of the shell. But, lest one be fooled by the many and prevailing misconceptions about love, it is essential to acquire at the earliest opportunity as much understanding as possible about the nature of genuine love.

SECTION III

The Nature of Genuine Love

The best description of genuine love that I know of is the famous passage in the thirteenth chapter of Paul's first letter to the Corinthians. It is best because it conforms best with the reality, with actual experiences that can come after the preparations indicated above, or their equivalent. Practical observations on how to make a beginning will be discussed in the final section of this book. It is possible that this chapter was quoted by Paul from some original author, one who obviously had a very unusual understanding of the real nature of love, for it seems to interrupt the continuity of the preceding and following passages and to stand out in contrast to them. Be that as it may, it shows a very deep and wonderful insight. It is interpreted well by Henry Drummond in *The Greatest Thing in the World.* But that passage is not meant to be read merely to enthuse over its poetic and philosophic beauty. If its meanings are taken really seriously they should be exceedingly alarming, because they show that our usual practices are not merely far below but are actually opposed. They show that genuine love is incompatible with all forms of egocentricity, with pride, with possessiveness or the assertion of "rights" over others, with jealousy, impatience, suspicions, and all kinds of inconsiderateness.

This incompatibility applies not only in relation to a particular person or persons singled out to be "loved," but toward all persons. Genuine love changes the inner feelings so that such negative attitudes no longer seem reasonable alternatives anywhere, and favoritism is eliminated. Once genuine love is experienced, none of the positive practices characteristic of it can seem an impossible ideal, and all become part of the most basic common sense. The social admonitions of the Founder of Christianity become meaningfully obvious, as do the examples of uplifting guidance furnished by many other great religious and humanitarian leaders.

Aside from the trivialities to which the term "love" is inappropriately applied, it nearly always refers, in modern society, just as inappropriately, to either romanticized lust or the interlocking of reciprocal egocentricities. It is sometimes applied, also misleadingly, to philanthropy or charity, the inaccuracy of this application being clearly shown in the chapter cited above (verse 3): "Though I give all I have to feed the poor but do not have genuine love, it accomplishes nothing." It really means *nothing*, no good, not even just a little, for charity without genuine love causes resentment, or pauperizes, or both, which is seriously damaging. The terminology has also been confused by the translation in the King James version of the word for "love" as "charity." *Caritas* is more meaningfully rendered by its English equivalents *dearness* or *caring*.

Perhaps an even more damaging tendency in religious circles has been to put aside genuine love by calling it divine love, assuming it to be only appropriate between God and man, in contrast to human love, as if it were not possible to experience it in relations with humans, as if it were not the main business of life to so learn from it about the nature of Ultimate Reality. The Judeo-Christian commandments to love God and to love one's neighbor do not involve two different kinds of love, but two applications of the same love. John, in his General Epistle (4:20), makes it very plain: "He that loveth not his brother whom he hath seen, how can he love God whom he hath not seen?" A neighbor is anyone close to you, and if you have a growing receptivity toward Ultimate Reality and are therefore capable of genuine love, you will often find a special neighbor in one who shares with you that receptivity, who is spiritually near, no matter how far away physically. The contrast, subconsciously felt and usually intended to be expressed in discussions about the two kinds of love, is really the contrast between genuine love and the elation of pursuing interlocking egocentricities, or the romanticized lust which people commonly confuse with human love.

Genuine love in personal relationships is so much the most wonderful experience that anyone can have, bringing such a deep, rich joy, lastingly and increasingly, that once anyone has really experienced it, he strives to make it replace all other kinds of relationships. He naturally acquires a loving openness toward everyone with whom he comes into close contact, being especially sensitive, aware, and receptive to the good qualities in each person, though at the same time not unaware of bad qualities (whether subordinate or predominant), and is always on the lookout for ways to help people get free from their self-limitations. This does not mean that he feels superior, for he is also aware of these problems in himself. Nor does it mean that he treats everyone alike, for physical circumstances and the varying degrees of receptivity in different persons limit his opportunities, much as in a cooperative game of "catch," where the return of the ball by the other participants is needed if the game is to go on.

Genuine love is naturally and beautifully expressed by physical affection, where appropriate, as well as in many other ways. In actual application, genuine love does not do anything inappropriate, "doth not behave itself unseemly;" but what is really appropriate may have little to do with the mechanical rules of modern society, which are so inaccurate that they produce results the very opposite of what are intended. Real affection is much too often held back by artificial rules based on the prevalence of egocentricities. We have polluted the beautiful command: "Love thy neighbor as thyself," by qualifying it with the cautious warning: "unless thy neighbor be an attractive member of the opposite sex ineligible for courting." To be sure, nearly everyone in our society is strongly egocentric, and so, showing affection to an attractive neighbor is likely to result in romantic-lust exploitation (often mutual), which in the long run is degrading and undesirable, hence to be avoided. But this way of putting the qualification makes no allowance for the rare but vitally important occurrences of genuine love, which it is the main business of life to promote. We should instead think, for qualification: be sure it is genuine love! Be sure that it is not an excitement that you "fall into," but the exercise of a capacity you have developed by overcoming your own egocentricities and acquiring an awareness of and receptivity to the good in other persons.

Though affection is a natural expression of love in appropriate circumstances, it cannot be taken as proof or indication of love, for in our society it is nearly always motivated (without realizing it) by romanticized lust or by reciprocating egocentricities, or (brazenly and with full realization) by an overt desire to exploit. Expressions of affection have been natural and frequent among higher animals, early men, and less inhibited moderns, not only toward the young but toward adults as well, as in the grooming of Primates. But when affection is really motivated by genuine love and is truly felt, it is a joy unimaginable until that kind has been experienced, and it is always appropriate, unless in the presence of others it risks too seriously the activation of their egocentricities.

Though it is possible to have genuine love for persons of any age and of any sex, and one who is ready for it tries to be as little as possible influenced by favoritism or by favoritism shown him, still he usually has a better chance of experiencing real love for the first time with an attractive member of the opposite sex. The powerful extra incentives assist him, as Jesus pointed out, quoting the Old Testament to the effect that God "made them male and female." When there is something that our customary social training makes so difficult that hardly anyone can do it, attempts to do it without all the help available are extreme folly or braggadocio, not at all consistent with the humility that inherits the earth. But proof that the experience is of the genuine kind must be looked for in an increasingly sympathetic, understanding, loving attitude toward all others. A person who has conscientiously striven and has successfully overcome his egocentricities, and so has grown up to the capacity for genuine love, should be able to be glad about himself and about his attractive neighbor and about all others who show any receptivity toward reality, and even about all those others who do not, for he knows that there lies in each a hidden potential for receptivity which he might be able to bring out if happily he can see an opportunity to get through to it under especially favorable circumstances, though it will require his utmost skill at the right time and place.

Martin Buber puts it another way. The usual attitude of people in our society toward persons, things, or ideas he calls an "I-it" attitude (or relationship), in which you consider only the utility or satisfaction that you may obtain, as opposed to the "I-Thou" attitude (or relationship), in which you become fully receptive to and appreciative of the reality of that which confronts you for its own sake, forgetting yourself. As your awareness of and appreciation of (your genuine love for) many individual realities, or "Thou's," grows, they all together add up to an awareness or approach to Ultimate Reality, to an enthusiasm for, or worship of the Great Thou, or God.

The intense joy, or ecstasy, of the first and all subsequent relationships of this kind opens up a whole new continent or a new world to explore, as yet known to hardly any persons in our society. You may do many of the same things you would have done otherwise, but with a very different feeling. Duties that contribute to constructive results cease to be burdensome tasks, for they are lightened by the joy of doing them for love. Only activities that interfere with more valuable accomplishments remain or become undesirable, causing one to strive to switch his occupations to more effective pursuits. But genuine love is always patient, because it is sustained by joy in the heart. It knows from experience that contributing to the long-run welfare and happiness of another person or persons is the only way to attain the highest level of intense and lasting joy. It knows that this is done naturally by services, by expressing love in actions and manners, in understanding and trust, and by tactfully trying to help the other person or persons to get over their limitations, even through inducing them to get free from the current social system of interlocking egocentricities in favor of following the path of genuine love themselves.

It should be easy to recognize the presence or absence of genuine love in yourself or in others by whether there is a lack of negative attitudes and behavior, and even more by whether there are many well-developed positive ones. There should be a complete lack or almost complete lack of negative emotions (jealousy, envy, touchiness or negative sensitivity, resentment, vindictiveness, anger, hate, cowardice); a lack of expressions of egocentric competitiveness (possessiveness, pride, vanity, boastfulness, gladness when others go wrong, which is due to a desire to feel superior or to be justified in doing wrong yourself, or in doing poorly); an absence of self-indulgence (slothfulness, lust, overeating, or eating the wrong things, or excessive use of stimulants); and a lack of signs of personal weakness (irritability, inconsiderateness, excessive criticism, boredom, dishonesty, cruelty, or any form of taking unfair advantage). For a time there may be a few remnants of the hard cores of some of these things, but they should be fast melting away. On the other hand, there will be the many positive qualities that lead to discernment and understanding and happy personal relations: receptivity, humility, patience, appreciation, sympathy, trustfulness, non-competitive generosity, good temper, courtesy, kindness, readiness to encourage, sincerity—both emotional and intellectual,—hopefulness, faith, courage, diligence, perseverance, endurance, joyfulness. The development of many of these qualities prior to an experience of genuine love is difficult and requires much energy, but along with such an experience they become natural and comparatively easy.

People who are still motivated by self-limiting egocentricity are easily fooled by shallow imitations of love. They overemphasize in themselves the constructive qualities which they may have and minimize or even justify or commend the destructive ones. Hence they count themselves as loving, and imagine others with similar attitudes are, too, for they cannot think a much higher level of feeling is possible for normal people, and often they see little or nothing wrong in those who are irresponsible, selfish, possessive, vain, vindictive, etc., if only such persons make a special point of being nice to *them*, especially those whom they can exploit in order to exercise their romanticized lusts. That is why it is said that "love" is blind. In most cases they prefer these reciprocating egocentrics also because they do not challenge them to take a step forward toward reality. On the other hand, anyone who has experienced enough genuine love so that it has become the controlling influence in his life will easily recognize others who have developed a capacity for it, and will welcome them enthusiastically, distinguishing them easily from egocentric imitations (except perhaps for service stars) and will be assisted by their challenge to go forward.

Nevertheless, the one who has genuine love will apply his patience to all those who are limited by their shells, including those who are making valiant efforts to get free, though subject to frequent setbacks, and those who are more or less amiable but are making little or no effort to get out, and also really obnoxious and bad people. He will understand the causes of their being like that and sympathize with the severe unpleasantness which they suffer on account of it, or will suffer in trying to get free, merely because they have cut themselves off from all the really inspiring experiences in life. This does not mean that a creative, loving person will be sentimentally oblivious of the dangerous aspects of unscrupulous people, so that he will let himself get trapped into positions where he can be taken advantage of (that would be an unkindness to them, tempting them), but he will be constantly looking for ways to help them, kindly and tactfully, even if only a little at a time, out of the courses that are leading them toward their emotional dungeons and torture chambers. In contrast, egocentric people tend to react in kind toward such persons, if they are not specially favored by them, and so become themselves victims of more negative feelings toward these types, hating, trying to get even, being envious, resentful, or haughty and exclusive. Negative feelings do the most harm to the ones who have them, unless they succeed in arousing similar reactions on the part of their victims or intended victims.

Moreover, a person with genuine love will not be so gentle in trying to help people out of their limitations that they are not affected by it, but he will be persistent in urging a step forward, even when it encounters typical resistance, slowing down only enough to avoid the danger of losing effectual influence, in contrast to egocentric people who care little whether others make fundamental progress or not if only they continue to provide opportunities for the furtherance of the egocentric's own life strategy. Genuine people help others, or try to, because of the joy they experience in helping and in promoting the others' long-run happiness and welfare, without considering the possibilities of any other kind of return, whereas egocentrics, if they are helpful, do so in order to get commendation or return favors or to put other people down, and if their plans seem to be heading for success, they may become enthusiastic about them (though that is different from real, lasting joy).

One who is acquiring the capacity for genuine love will be not only appreciative and receptive toward the good in other persons and in nature, but he will be also open and eager to have his own inaccuracies or misconceptions corrected, to have his own egocentric pattern or patterns exposed, and to be helped to free himself from them. As he grows more able to recognize persons who are genuine, who have constructive aims and want to help, he becomes more trustful and enthusiastic, welcomes their advances and their efforts to help, and allows himself to be happy in doing so. Thus he becomes better able to "believe all things" that have good in them, that are tied to reality, because he is in less danger of being deluded by wishful thinking about supposed good things. He has more faith. He is also more communicative, both because he has less to hide and because he is more trustful, more inclined to recognize that the other person wants to be and is capable of understanding, and thus he is more willing to make continuing efforts to help him get the right idea.

In contrast, the person who is still on the level of

the present world social order will tend to keep his most precious thoughts to himself, often subconsciously suspecting that they have some weaknesses, and at the same time overemphasizing the self-serving motivation or stupidity of others, whom he is too ready to believe prone to "misunderstand." Sometimes he says "Never mind," meaning, "How can I expect such as you to understand?" There is a deficiency of trust and love. He is usually on the defensive and highly suspicious of anyone who tries to help him climb to a higher level of living, for he fears it may require him to make an extra effort or to give up some of his selfish or egocentric interests. Hence he usually dislikes or is cool toward such a person. He will often be unaware or oblivious and consequently unappreciative of persons, ideas, and even things (objects, landscapes, nature in general) except when they coincide with an interest with which he identifies, or when he wants to know about opponents in order to overcome or thwart them (if they interfere with his interests, or he thinks they do). He is typically possessive, insisting on his rights and privileges and on the rights and privileges of those on whom he depends or with whom he identifies. He tends to show favoritism, expecting to get it returned.

Adults, being more sophisticated, are more successful than children in camouflaging these traits, but they hold on to them, often more strongly, under cover. They don't openly and arbitrarily demand: "I want this; I want that. I don't like this; I don't like that," insisting on and trying to enforce their own way. They don't boast so much about how good they are, or those with whom they identify, exaggerating beyond the reality that they are right, their things in better order, or they know a better way. But the children have learned all these things from adults, directly or through other children, or because adults were not able or did not take the trouble to show them something better. Hence they grow up to be rigid, obstinate, resentful, inconsiderate, callous, even sometimes intentionally cruel. Because of some or all of these attitudes of childhood and adulthood, nearly all adults lead lives with very little genuine love, lives which as a consequence tend to become more and more dull and dreary, full of increasingly burdensome duties, difficulties, disappointments, and discouragements.

Fortunately this dreary scene is relieved here and there by touches of better attitudes, and once in a while by a bursting through of some real inspiration. In fact, everyone must have at least a small amount of genuine love, expressed in good feelings, or he would go mad. Regrettably, the average in our society is very low. Those who are above the average are the pleasant, agreeable people. There are a few far above it but hardly ever far enough for it to be a continuing and controlling influence. Inside the shell there is always a beautiful person, the divine core or center, and in different persons all of these are of equal worth, though they are not of equal accessibility. It is usually easier to see through the shells of very young children, for they are so much thinner and softer than the shells of nearly all adults.

To develop the capacity for genuine love it is important to begin with someone, whether child or adult, with whom you can be aware directly of this equality of worth. The adult who is sufficiently qualified is able to perceive through the child's thin shell his glorious potentials, and to perceive in another adult, through holes or thin places in the thicker shell, positive characters equally worthy of great enthusiasm. The child nearly always has physical attractiveness, and that helps tremendously to inspire the leap forward which is necessary to see the first person through the eyes of genuine love. Physical, as well as other kinds of attractiveness, are big factors in making possible the first breakthrough of this kind toward an adult. Mistakenly conscientious feelings of guilt over being influenced by these should not be allowed to interfere. The important point is that the first experience of this kind is so difficult in our society that it is hardly ever attained, and so nothing should be allowed to interfere and all aids should be encouraged. Temptations to romanticize lust must of course be ruled out, and this can be done, as will be more fully explained later, by making sure that the relationship develops on an all-round balanced basis.

To participate in such an experience and maintain a feeling of equality, an adult needs to work hard to overcome in himself any serious deficiencies which would tempt the other person to feel superior, such as a frivolous or scatter-brained or lazy, undeveloped intellect, or a coarse, crude, ill-mannered, or unclean personage. Later, when the capacity for genuine love has been more fully developed, at least potential equality can be recognized in spite of any deficiencies. Physical and mental handicaps, whether they can be overcome or not, are then no longer an obstacle, and handicapped persons are often aided by being especially receptive. Sometimes handicapped persons have their best opportunities for genuine love, with a complete feeling of equality, in other persons equally handicapped but in a complementary way, so that each can supply the deficiency of the other. For complete equality, there must be no condescension and no flattery or susceptibility to flattery. Toward all persons, anyone with an enlarged capacity for real love and joy can become genuinely humble, seeking like water to accommodate to each situation, interested in participating in any program that may be helpful to bring out real truth, hopeful for new things while still appreciating what is valid in the old, ready to see the good in what the other person offers, to relieve tensions, lessen conflicts, and spread abroad lasting enjoyment, each of these activities tending to make him happy. Thus what formerly seemed to be duties toward other persons turn into joys, and the loving person is thoroughly happy inside in spite of opposition, misunderstandings, and problems that keep cropping up, which merely add a touch of sadness or regret that they should still be so.

Because of my training and experience, I am more familiar with the Judeo-Christian evidence of reality than I am with the constructive elements which I feel must surely be present, and to some extent have found, in the world's other religions. I must take my examples from what I know best, and trust that others will recognize similar features in their own backgrounds, no matter how differently expressed. I know that the heart and core of the teachings of Jesus is genuine love, and although some outstanding individuals here and there, and probably more obscure humble ones, have caught its spirit in varying degrees, it is obvious that no nation, no community, not even any church has really grasped its meaning and made it the controlling influence. Jesus kept trying to tell what it would be like, in His parables about the Kingdom of Heaven (in Matthew) and the Kingdom of God (as it is also called, mostly in the other Gospels), a society in which genuine love is the controlling influence. It is a state of being that can be realized right here and now, not one to be attained by dying. Compare Mark 1:15, and: "Blessed are the poor in spirit, for theirs *is* the Kingdom of Heaven" (they already have it, as Phillips puts it). "The Kingdom of God *is* within you (or among you)." Some "will not taste death before they have seen the Kingdom of God already come in power." We are taught to pray: "Thy Kingdom come . . . on earth as it is in heaven." Indeed, if it is not experienced here, it is doubtful if it would be any easier to attain somewhere else.

These parables emphasize its supreme importance and the necessity of sacrificing everything that cannot be subordinated to it. It is the pearl of great price and the treasure hidden in the field, worthy of selling everything else to receive the joy it brings. Everything opposed to it must be cut out, even though it be as much a part of you and as dear to you as your right eye or your right arm or your own egocentric self-limiting pattern. The cares of this world, including the over-emphasis on money or on any material thing (which moth and rust and the erosion of time destroy) and also commonplace or fashionable non-productive or trivial activities, and even many conventionally held obligations to family, friends, or society as a whole, are symbolized by the thorn bushes that spring up to choke out the seed of growing understanding of reality and the experience of genuine love. It is not only the Prodigal who before his reform wastes his assets with frivolities and lust, but also the Elder Brother who, like good church people unaware of and inexperienced in genuine love (love different from the gratification of egocentric aims and even different from altruism), misses the Kingdom of Heaven.

But sometimes, like the tares among the wheat, some of the distracting influences must be tolerated temporarily until the time is ripe for the harvest, the breaking-out from the interlocking network of worldly egocentricities, provided that valid plans are made to subordinate or eliminate them, always giving wholeheartedly first priority to the establishment of the Kingdom of Heaven. One cannot afford to look back longingly at the egocentric snares, or to hold on to some of them, lest the opportunity missed leaves a life of such great disappointments as to build up from the tears it causes a pillar of salt, as in the case of the Old Testament allegory of the wife of Lot, quoted by Jesus. According to the traditional system of Jesus' time the burial of a deceased father was considered one of the most pressing obligations a man could have, and yet when a decisive step toward the new way of living was needed, Jesus indicated there was not time then to say farewell to family and friends or even to bury the father. He said, "Let the dead bury the dead." Those who are enwrapped in the egocentric system and so are not alive to reality can take care of things that need to be left behind.

If anyone wishes to become really alive ("save his life"), he must give up his self-limiting entanglements ("lose his life," or what has become his life) for the sake of what Jesus stood for—a new society in which genuine love has the controlling influence. There must be a drastic change. You cannot usefully sew a piece of unshrunk cloth onto an old garment or put new wine in old wineskins. You cannot enter into a strong man's house unless you first bind the strong man (your egocentricities). You must be "poor in spirit," not so satisfied with yourself that you are unwilling to work hard against your egocentricities. You must be aware of your spiritual needs. It is almost impossible for a rich man (one who is spiritually satisfied with himself) to enter the Kingdom of Heaven. To feed the materially poor is praiseworthy and is usually done with good intentions, as something a loving person wants to do when he can, though it sometimes leads to dependence or to an increase in the population, so that in time more people are hungry than before. But to feed the spiritually poor, those who are receptive, helping and encouraging them to develop more of a capacity for genuine love, is a much greater service, for it will not only increase happiness and well-being and the number of people who are being helpful, but it will also thereby reduce the waste of natural resources (for real joys require fewer resources) and in time reduce the number of people who are hungry.

"No man can serve two masters"; he cannot seek to bring out Ultimate Reality, expressed in genuine love, and concurrently or alternately serve his own egocentricity (mammon, in the older translations). To narrow the meaning of these sayings to money alone, or even to just material things, is to belittle their significance and miss most of the main point. You have only to read on a little in the passages indicated to see that Jesus didn't mean just money, that He was using whatever term He used symbolically to represent a much wider meaning, as He often did. Of course it included the wrong attitude toward money, and covetousness in general, the indulgence of lust, and many other manifestations of egocentricity. He concludes by saying that if, in contrast to worldly men (indicating some esteemed churchmen and others), you have the right attitude in your heart and thus give first priority to, "seek first the Kingdom of God," all legitimate lesser things will come as a matter of course. His other remarks about rich men and the materially poor whom you have "always with you" should also be regarded in this light, and these problems should be subordinated to the importance of positive feeling, which is broader, and will take care of them, too.

Jesus expected that once people began to experience the Kingdom of Heaven, or Paradise on Earth, it would spread like wildfire, would grow like a mustard seed into a big tree with large branches, so that the birds of the air (in those days representing to the Jews symbolically the Gentiles) could make nests in its shade, and would permeate the mass of mankind like the leaven that a woman hid in three measures of meal. Why not? Once you have the right idea, it is easy (Matt. 11:28-30), and it brings joy (Mark 2:19). But many are invited to the banquet and few come (Luke 14:16-24), because they are distracted by many other interests. There must be a complete commitment (Luke 14:28-31). It is not enough to drive out the distractions, for an empty house will soon fill with more (Luke 11:24-26; Matt. 12:43-45). There must be a positive experience of genuine love. Although small groups of Christians seem to have caught some of this spirit in the form of a beloved fellowship and preserved it during the first three centuries of the Christian Era, it was dissipated when Christianity became the official religion of the Empire (see Gerald Heard: *The Social Substance of Religion*). Even so, it is doubtful if many of the earliest Christians fully understood and experienced what Jesus was talking about. His prescription really has not been tried. It is still possible for Jesus' prophecy to come true if we can apply, with a fuller understanding of reality and the right feelings, the directions He plainly gave.

Many people think they know what genuine love is, but unless they have experienced it, they do not know; and unless they exhibit all its main features, including those described above, and have eliminated the egocentric ones, they have not experienced it. A romance that ends in divorce or merely simmers down to routine cooperation is no more based on genuine love than is a wild affair. Real love must broaden out to a changed attitude toward all people. It is best to get it while still very young, but if not then, the sooner the better. Nothing else is worthy to take precedence over it, so far as personal relations are concerned. Even during business hours, when you are making your main contribution to the running of the community, or preparing for it (in school, factory, office, running the household, etc.) there are often opportunities for improving personal attitudes and, in solitary occupations, thought. Much of what has been said above has been said many, many times, but it remains to be recognized that now it must be taken seriously and in its entirety, if the human race is to survive. No halfway measures will do. Hence the following section will discuss our opportunities for finding a new and vastly improved way of living, based on the actual experience of genuine love. These are guidelines to experiences not usually imagined to be possible, but since current trends show them to be necessary for human survival, careful investigation discloses that they are indeed possible and offer opportunities for the richest rewards.

Modification of Practices in Modern Society to Bring Out More of the Kind of Love that Is So Much Needed

Opportunity to experience and so to understand genuine love exists for all persons during all stages of their lives, only most people do not know about it. It is not confined to the youthful years when romanticized lust is strongest. Jesus makes this most plain when He is explaining the Kingdom of Heaven by the parable of the Laborers in the Vineyard. Those who do not come in until the eleventh hour of the day are treated exactly like those who came in at the first. Only, if you come in to a better way of living (where the grapes are) early in life, you may participate in the joy of it through all your life, while those who come in late have missed much. The work is not really laborious, except for those who have not caught the real spirit of it, like the Pharisees of that time and some of the corresponding modern professing churchmen and still egocentric do-gooders.

The entrance requirement is as stated in the first Beatitude: "Blessed are the poor in spirit: for theirs is the Kingdom of Heaven." It is necessary first to be willing to acknowledge one's own deficiency on account of egocentricity, whether easily discernible or subtle, and then make strenuous efforts to wear the egocentric shell thin or make holes in it. When this has been done, one becomes ready and receptive to genuine love and can safely participate in it. In terms of the parable, you have to be in a state of mind in which nothing else has "hired" you. (See Gerald Heard's explanation of the first Beatitude in his *Code of Christ*, Chapter 2.)

When you have at least partly qualified, there are many situations even now in our society in which it is possible to begin to experience genuine love, and it should also be possible to enlarge these opportunities greatly and facilitate participation in them. I shall describe some of them, taking them up mostly in the order of the stages in the individual's life cycle.

Probably the relationship which can be most gloriously developed in this way, with the most creative results, is the close, personal, genuine love relationship between an older person and a very young child (one in his pre-teens). It is the opportunity specifically recommended by Jesus in the strongest possible terms. It is the first one that I experienced as an adult and found to be amazingly effective in producing a beneficial uplift. And Jesus "took a child, and put him in the midst of them; and taking him in his arms, he said to them: 'Whoever receives one such child in my name receives me; and whoever receives me, receives not me but him who sent me. . . . Let the children come to me, do not hinder them; for to such belongs the Kingdom of God. Truly I say to you, whoever does not receive the Kingdom of God like a child shall not enter it.' And he took them in his arms and blessed them, laying his hands upon them" (Mark 9:36-37 and 10:14-16).

It was not Jesus' custom to say more than He meant nor to stress merely superficial or mechanical actions. This and similar passages appear in all three of the Synoptic Gospels. When He took the little children in His arms and blessed them, He did not merely run His fingers around their heads in the form of a halo, or pat their heads, and say "I bless you." He really loved them, and they loved Him back. Nor did He say that He alone could do such things, but rather He repeatedly said: "Follow me," and (Phillips' translation) "The man who believes in me will do the same things that I have done" (John 14:12). There cannot be anything more important than this, for "Whoever receives one such child in my name receives me; and whoever receives me, receives not me but him who sent me...." "For I go to the Father." He is on the way to Ultimate Reality; and he who receives the little child in the spirit of Jesus will also begin to be aware of the deeper reality.

What does it mean to receive a little child, to become receptive to him (or her), to have an "I-Thou" attitude? It does *not* mean to become sentimental, to say "Oh, the sweet little darling," to fondle the child and then say "Now run along and play." It surely means that we are to be deeply moved and learn something of great importance. He said: "I thank thee, O Father, Lord of heaven and earth, that thou hast hid these things from the wise and prudent, and hast revealed them unto babes: even so, Father, for so it seemed good in thy sight" (Matt. 11:25-26; and Luke 10:21). We cannot learn calculus or political strategy from little children. What we can learn from them, and it is of great importance, is genuine love, for they have a potential for it. It comes right up from their biologic roots, the product of hundreds of millions of years of biologic progress. As Wordsworth said, they come "trailing clouds of glory . . . from God who is our home." We can draw it out of them by being truly receptive. That is what education really means, to draw out (from *e*, out; and *duc*, lead or draw, draw out—not stuff in). This is not mere theory or impossible idealism. I know from my own experience that it really works. The adult can learn what genuine love is from the little ones, and in so doing help them to develop their potential while it is still easy for them, before their shells close around them in their early teens and it becomes much more difficult.

It means developing a close, personal, one-to-one genuine love relationship, as intense and meaningful as an adult love relationship is generally expected to be. It must be an all-round balanced relationship, with affection balanced by genuine interest, sharing of activities, sympathy, appreciation, awareness of the child's beauty, freshness, enthusiasm, and unlimited potentials, and correspondingly a disclosure to the child of the adult's having achieved some openness to reality with which he can be helpful, of his finding his joy in promoting the child's long-run welfare and happiness, so that the child is encouraged to respond further in kind. It is a reciprocal or mutual feedback process.

The possibility of achieving a really wonderful relationship of this kind, capable of creating a new kind of life on a higher level, as it is meant to be, has been overlooked in our society because of the traditional taboo against developing it between an adult and a child of the opposite sex. This is based upon a well-founded fear of lustful exploitation by adult males, and upon an aversion to more or less motherly smothering by egocentric adult females. That is why only qualified adults who have made substantial progress toward overcoming their egocentricities should try it, and comprehensive precautions should be taken to prevent abuses. If these requirements are observed, however, the most effective procedure for promoting the child's best development through to adulthood can be made very much safer, as well as more constructive, than the present largely misleading practices could ever be. The really great improvement, which we all see is needed, is bound to require a significant change in our customs as great as this. The extra incentive of sexual attraction, which is already active between the ages of six and twelve, is needed to inspire the enthusiasm on both sides that will lift the relationship far above what has been the usual experience.

Group leaders of the same sex, like Scout leaders, are valuable and have their place; and a man and a boy or a woman and little girl may find a very meaningful participation in common interests; but the added joy of personal tenderness, consideration, and inspiration between the sexes generates energy of a different order of magnitude, which can accomplish what hardly anything else ever can. What we are trying to do is something far above even the best of ordinary experience. Think back and recall the characteristics described in the section on genuine love. They are not just amiable ideals. They are all essentials, else you do not have genuine love. Yet in common experience when there is only a little of some of them, it is called "love." There are many forms of friendly cooperation that are highly desirable, but not sufficient to lift society up to a new level. For that there must be the application of every creative means available. God "made them male and female" not just for the mixing of genes but for the integration of qualities that make reality whole. Nothing commonplace in our present tradition and experience can be sufficient.

Some influence of this sort can be supplied by the parents or those who are in the position of parents, but they have natural handicaps, which means that usually someone outside of the immediate family will be needed. They have a very important role to fill, and it is essential for the welfare of the child that they fill it well. They need to look out for the child's physical health, to provide him with discipline (so that discipline is not a problem to him), to give him tasks to do, without monetary compensation, so that he may share in the family endeavor, and all this must be done with as much real love as they can muster, giving time, attention, interest, and encouragement, and planning treats which will further, or at least not interfere with, the child's long-run welfare. Yet, even with the best they can do, they have serious handicaps, because it is very difficult for them not to be egocentrically possessive (which is incompatible with real love), because they are so accustomed to bossing the children around, and because they appear so familiar and routine to the children that they seldom can capture active spiritual imaginations (inspire with charisma). It is very hard for parents not to be aware of all the time, effort, and money put into the raising of their children, not to justify counting them as assets from whom to expect a return, and also to be free from egocentric concern for the reproduction and perpetuation of their own physical or social image.

Parents who spoil their children, giving them things that are not good for them, letting then get away with behavior that will cause them serious trouble later on, and not showing them the things in life that are of real value, are demonstrating a lack of love. They try to bribe the children into liking them or into not giving them any trouble, and they end up with a generation gap—children who have little or no regard for them, causing more and more trouble. Children who have been allowed to have their own way most of the time are bound to be unhappy, a little at first, but more and more through their whole lives. They can have no idea of the long-run values which are most important, especially ones that require less interesting preparations or introductions, and so they miss all of them; they also miss many immediate values; and they get involved in wrong courses, the ultimate costs of which they cannot even imagine.

The kind of "love" that most children have for their parents is what C. S. Lewis, in his *The Four Loves*, calls "need-love." Lewis confuses the picture by supposing that "need-love" is the only kind that you can have for God, and therefore he concludes that it must be real love; but that is not so, for if you get a healthy understanding of the wonderfulness of Reality you can have real love, in the form of enthusiastic appreciation and the joy of conforming to it and of bringing others to it. "Gift-love," as he describes it, or altruism, is also inferior to the joy of inducing others to share and participate, with all the personal involvement that circumstances allow. There is only one kind of real love. Children who have been led astray by our social customs seldom have much of the real love for their parents, which expresses itself in helping to do chores or to save trouble by being careful with their own things and with others' for the joy of doing it, rather than for the praises or rewards it earns. They do, however, enjoy the comforts of cuddling and of belonging, of feeling secure. Parents, who usually insist that they "love" their children, may also have satisfaction in cuddling, but after the children reach school age seldom have much more than the temporary satisfactions of possessiveness and of reciprocating egocentricities. These usually involve elation at the child's coming to them with "need-love" and may include the interlocking of star and clinging vine patterns (either way round). The nero-turtle axis is seldom mistaken for love. Women often have more real love for infants and toddlers of pre-school age (or pre-nursery-school age), especially during the time of the original "We." They may retain something of this in later life, and that may be why (until lately) they have been psychologically less unbalanced than men and have tended to live longer under protected conditions.

A time comes, usually during elementary school years (ages 6 to 12), when children need to begin to get experience in relating to someone outside of the immediate family, for as soon as they reach their teens they will become drastically exposed to it, and they had better be prepared. During the pre-teen span, children seldom are interested or ready to develop close personal one-to-one real love relationships with each other, and it would be unfortunate if they did. They may develop egocentric crushes, showing favoritism in return for favoritism shown them. In contrast, they are ready and eager to experience a new relationship with an adult who comes to them with a friendly appeal and no offending qualities. I have had close contact with many of them and they are all open and receptive, some much more than others, some only a little. I suppose if I should get to know a much larger and wider sample I would find a few who were already, because of adverse training or other circumstances, completely closed off by prematurely established egocentric shells. But normally the novelty arouses their interest and they feel the need for human relatedness, especially if the adult is qualified to express genuine love. Although the adult should be careful not to undermine the parents' form of disciplining or do anything injurious to the child's physical, mental, or emotional well-being, he can be free of most of the parents' burden of establishing discipline, imposing tasks, and providing necessities, and so he can concentrate more on happy experiences and guide the child toward bringing out the child's potential for genuine love.

Within the family, the obvious resource to draw upon for extra help is the grandparents, uncles or aunts, or other relatives, if any of them happen to be qualified, have time and interest to give, and live near enough to be able to be effective. In former times, when the older people lived with the family on the farm, it sometimes happened naturally that after they stopped doing so much of the hard work they had the leisure to pass on to the children some of the mature knowledge and feeling of reality that they had gained during their long lives. Even then, though, there were few who were qualified to give much of value, and now our egocentricity has intensified so much that we can't stand having the old people around too close to us. Also circumstances have made it possible to relegate them one way or other to special communities for elderly persons where children are not allowed as regular residents. There there are elaborate facilities for amusing the old people and making them think they are active while they wait around to die, but they do not know what they are missing. The development of an intimate personal love relationship with the children is one of the very most joyous experiences of a lifetime, and if they experienced it they would know they were continuing or even beginning to participate in life in an important way. Occasional visits are not enough. Most of them assume that anything better than their present condition is hopeless because of the circumstances and the attitudes of the parents, and also because of the social taboo against expressing enough real affection to build the relationship up to effective levels. Thus we are wasting most of what may be our most valuable social resource.

But a few older people are still in areas where there are children, and it is not necessary that they be members of the family. Adoptive parents can do as good a job in bringing up children as natural parents, and so honorary grandparents, aunts, uncles, or just respected and properly qualified friends can do just as good a job as natural relatives. The important point is the qualification. Have they led conscientiously constructive lives, and have they made real progress in wearing their egocentric shells thin or opening holes in them? Really bad people often belong to families, and their belonging to the family does nothing to qualify them, while really good, well-qualified people can often spread priceless treasures among the children of a number of families not their own. Jesus did not confine His attentions offered to children merely to ones in his own family. A bachelor or maiden aunt may not be as well-qualified as one who has helped to raise a family of his (or her) own, but each should be appraised according to his individual qualifications.

A person who can be recognized as well-qualified

should be invited into the home and encouraged to relate to the children in his best and most capable way. If this is done under the parents' immediate supervision and with their cooperation, there is very little danger of abuse. A qualified, conscientious adult trying to bring out a child's capacity for real love is not going to molest the child. The horrors of neglected children left alone by parents and accosted in parks or other places by unbalanced strangers, or of ones kidnapped, which is all that many people seem to be able to think of in this connection, are not really relevant at all. Instead, the properly qualified adult would offer additional protection; and the risks of misjudging a person of good reputation who is being thoroughly supervised in the home are slight.

The qualified adult can help the child find out from actual experience what really counts in life, so that by the time he reaches his teens he will be proof against the problems that in the present social scene are otherwise so often overwhelming. If this is not done, nearly all children reach their teens with vacuums in their hearts and such strong drives to fill those vacuums that they fall for activities most unlikely to be of benefit and almost certain to do serious lasting damage to their lives, and in some cases can even lead to their premature deaths. When they arrive thus as emotional cripples they are worse off than physical cripples who have lost one or more arms, legs, eyes, etc., whereas it should be evident that serious dangers to pre-teens from malfunctioning of the program recommended here would, in comparison, scarcely ever arise. Which of the following is the more likely to do serious damage to a child: a supervised, responsible, conscientious, qualified adult, striving lovingly to reveal to the pre-teen-ager the real values of life, or an unsupervised teenager or group of teenagers who have not yet experienced responsibility, who have grown to distrust the guidance of adults, who know little or nothing of real love, who look to each other for compelling values, and are ready to experiment ignorantly with social dynamite? The latter are the ones whom the child who has been brought up without being allowed to experience the real values in life will in most cases seek out, as soon as he can insist on the modern freedoms of the teens!

Aside from the need to have the development of this intimate personal relationship with the child take place under the close supervision of parent or guardian, the exact procedure will have to be adjusted to the characteristics of each particular child and his situation, and in accordance also with the abilities, the ingenuity, and the inspiration of the adult, generated and stimulated by growing love. The relationship should be as broad and as diversified as possible. Reading aloud is one of the most effective activities, for it involves sharing a wide range of imagined experiences that can be chosen from really great sources, selected because of their constructive insight as well as their interest to the child, and the process can usually be enhanced by the shared joy of sympathetic and affectionate physical contact. The adult may hold the young child in his lap or close beside him on the sofa. However, the expressions of affection he offers tentatively should be continued only so far as the child welcomes them. They should never be forced, nor should the adult plead for a response or urge more than the child is in the mood for. The reading aloud is not done because the child can't read or because it is difficult for him (if it is) but because the sharing is more fun, just as going to a show or doing any other thing with a valued companion is more fun than doing it alone, and because it builds up the relationship. It gives each participant a greater depth of vision, as when bifocal vision brings out the third dimension, for each sees through his own eyes, and also sympathetically through the eyes and from the point of view of the other.

If the child is very young or has not been used to

being read to, it usually helps to start by reading something simple and easy and captivating (because of rhyming or pictures or other embellishments), such as Dr. Seuss' *The Cat in the Hat,* even though it does not have any element of insight into reality in its theme, incidents, or feeling tone—just to get used to being read to. The more popular of Beatrix Potter's little books are good, simple adventure stories, with a good feeling tone and many charming pictures. Most of them are not too long to hold a young child's attention. Fairy stories that have been popular for many generations because they illustrate well important principles of living are good to read, such as *Cinderella, Sleeping Beauty, Snow White, The Fisherman and his Wife,* etc. The earlier versions of *Cinderella* have values the Disney version lacks, and vice versa. When the stepsisters are represented as also beautiful physically, though ugly in attitude, it is more meaningful, for that is what really counts. Genuine love's first kiss can waken a *Sleeping Beauty,* but it requires much more preparation on the part of the lover than mere observation of her beauty, and she also must have developed so much receptivity as to be on the verge of waking to love. A. A. Milne's *Winnie the Pooh* stories are valuable for their good feeling tone. Kenneth Grahame's *Wind of the Willows* also has a good feeling tone, and in addition an important mystical element, as suggested by the title.

The Sneetches and Other Stories by Dr. Seuss is as much fun for the children as the one of his books previously mentioned, and in addition, three out of the four stories in it bring out clearly very significant human relation principles: the foolishness of being snooty; of feeling you are better than the other fellow for superficial reasons, such as the color of your skin; the foolishness of wasting time being stubborn or obstinate when, as in the other stories too, there is so much more of value in being friends and having fun together; and in the last

story the tremendous value of discovering the importance of the other fellow's feelings, not just your own,
with its helpfulness toward overcoming fear and antagonism even toward the strange and unknown. Children like to read the same stories over and over many
times. If the simple principles in these stories become
familiar to them, it will do much to diminish the egocentric shells growing up around them, especially if the
adults in their families are familiar with the stories too
and, on particularly appropriate occasions, remind them
of the applications of the principles to their own experiences. Sympathetic awareness of other people's feelings
would lessen the severity of conflicts at all levels, even
including international wars.

With preliminary reading experiences, some children at six and most at eight become capable of listening
happily in a close personal fellowship situation to C. S.
Lewis' *Chronicles of Narnia.* That is true in a one-to-one
or a one-to-two or -three situation. In a larger group
situation the listeners have to be older to concentrate
and not miss the important points because of distractions
in the group which would cause them to lose interest.
The stories are exciting and entertaining for the children, after the somewhat slow preparatory introductions
in some of them that are a usual feature of longer
stories. Lewis' insight into reality shows more clearly in
his simplified other world (Narnia) than in the com-
plexities of our own. That is why, he explains elsewhere,
he uses this form to bring out the great truths he recog-
nizes.

Books are not really good for children unless they
are also good for adults of all ages, as these are. The
good feeling, the sensitive appreciation of nature, the
profound meaning, and the symbolism are evident to
the adult and can be pointed out to the child. Aslan, the
magnificent great lion, stands for genuine love, and his
actions and directions all along show how the Kingdom

of Heaven is to be approached. The White Witch, who makes it always winter and never Christmas in Narnia, stands for the egocentric limitations and social traditions in our world that keep out the warmth of genuine love and the spirit for which we celebrate Christmas, until she is overcome by Aslan with the significantly necessary help of the children. The Green Witch and serpent conform to the standard world-wide symbol for the lust that captivates humans from adolescence on, and the dreariness of the earthmen in her underground kingdom is an apt portrayal of what our world is like in contrast to what it could be.

The naturalness and vividness of the episodes where those who are more sensitive and aware, or have already experienced a small part of reality, acquire the ability to see Aslan and to see and believe in the rest of reality, are skillfully brought out; and to follow these episodes understandingly is truly thrilling. Such developing characters contrast realistically with the blindness and stupidity of those who are so shut up in the egocentric prisons of their own imaginings (avaricious schemings, fears of being duped, and vanity) that they misinterpret or cannot see and appreciate the beauty of reality all around them. At one point the egocentric shell of a participant grows so extreme that it becomes visible as a dragon skin encasing him, and the method of its eventual removal is psychologically very sound. There is so much beauty and wonderment in these stories that more of value comes out each time with numerous delightful rereadings. (Lewis' imaginative stories written for adults are also packed with thought-provoking meaning and entertaining suggestiveness.)

As C. S. Lewis credits much of his inspiration in writing imaginative stories for bringing out reality to George MacDonald, it is not surprising that MacDonald's children's stories have a similar quality of sympathetic human understanding and spiritual insight. *The Lost*

Princess is a gem for making clear to child and adult alike, in engrossing story, the self-infliction of egocentric growth, and the parents' temptations to produce it, with the joy of seeing how it can be overcome. The Curdie stories mingle appreciation and enthusiasm over deep goodness with the excitement of overcoming obstacles. *At the Back of the North Wind* is a story unusually permeated with such a good feeling tone that it is a continuous pleasure to read it; and *Sir Gibbie,* which does not make use of any imaginary shortcuts or simplifications and requires a more mature child to read it, is an amazingly sensitive and appreciative story of a really good, though handicapped, character.

Many writers can create realistic bad characters, but it requires a person with deep understanding to make a realistic good character, which both Lewis and Mac-Donald can do. Thoughtful older children, approaching teen age or in their early teens, who have caught the spirit of these other books can even share with an adult, enjoyably and with enlightening stimulation of the imagination, MacDonald's *Lilith,* written for adults and requiring some explanations by the adult, but with unlimited freedom of the imagination suggesting reality as in a poem. Especially revealing is the contrast between the little ones who retain their capacity for genuine love as they grow up and the ones who grow stupid from eating the bad fruit of egocentricity and who, like the people in our world, have to die in their egocentric entanglements and be reborn, sometimes requiring the most drastic treatment involving sorrow and bitterness (by the character Mara).

There are many other really good books for children in their upper pre-teens, valuable for adults as well, providing good entertainment and also uplifting experiences. The writings of Frances Hodgson Burnett speak for themselves. The Laura Ingalls Wilder *Little House* series is full of good family feeling and basic historical pioneer experience. Among the writings of Rudyard Kipling, special mention should be made of the Mowgli stories in *The Jungle Book,* and "The White Seal" with its quest for a better world; and in the *Just So Stories* "The Cat that Walked by Himself" and "The Butterfly that Stamped," though the latter may require more maturity to appreciate the feeling element in marital relations and the importance of not showing off. Kipling's natural history is atrocious, but his presentation of the attitudes of human beings in the form of animals is pleasingly enlightening. Many old-timers have lasted because of their quality: Louisa May Alcott's *Little Women,* etc., Eleanor Porter's *Pollyanna,* which is good in spite of the derogatory popular use of the name, and in the same vein Kate Douglas Wiggin's *Rebecca of Sunnybrook Farm,* Johanna Spyri's *Heidi,* unabridged, illustrating grandparent-child relationship; Jean Webster's *Daddy Longlegs,* Margaret Sidney's *Five Little Peppers,* L. M. Montgomery's *Anne of Green Gables,* Anna Sewell's *Black Beauty,* Marguerite Henry's *Justin Morgan Had a Horse,* and many more that can be selected because of their valid feeling qualities. Boys especially like Ernest Thompson Seton's *Wild Animals I Have Known.*

Lewis Carroll's *Alice in Wonderland* may require more maturity to appreciate its wit. The first of C. S. Lewis' space trilogy *Out of the Silent Planet* is within the range of pre-teenagers, but the second, *Perelandra,* gets involved in the middle with too much philosophy for most of them, and the last deals with vital issues much too complicated for them. As an introduction to somewhat archaic language and a well-known character, Howard Pyle's version of *Robin Hood* is good, or his story of *King Arthur and His Knights.* Reading one of these helps to prepare for the style and perspective of William Morris' *The Wood Beyond the World* in its original form, which is a love story illustrating the importance of developing an all-round relationship before expressing it in complete physical intimacy. Even the archaic *The Pilgrim's Progress* by John Bunyan is still valid in many ways, if allowance is made for some now outgrown misconceptions. C. S. Lewis' *The Pilgrim's Regress* is a symbolic updated view of this kind of thing. Gerald Heard's *Gabriel and the Creatures* has for its theme the important scientific record described in the first section of this book. Though clearly intended for children, it is easier for adults to understand, and they need to do some explaining. Some of the more advanced listeners may be up to appreciating the human sensitivity in James Barrie's beautiful love story *The Little Minister,* and that may serve as an introduction to the many other good Scotch stories. From there young listeners and readers are ready to pass on into the many more, good, fully adult books, especially those that have stood the test of time. There is never an age when reading aloud together does not enhance the value of reading through sharing. I have read many of these books, and even more, to a few youngsters, and some of them to about sixty, individually, and so can speak from experience as to the validity of the program.

Besides reading, there are many other activities that can help to build the needed, all-round balanced relationship. Some children have been pre-conditioned against being read to by some unfortunate experience or just plain childish prejudice. For them the relationship must be built by other means, for the reading should not be forced, though the adult should always be looking for and hoping for opportunities to break down the prejudice against this most helpful aid. Nearly all little children enjoy mild forms of gymnastics, and these are valuable for helping to break the ice toward establishing close, positive feeling relationships, if the adult is careful to be sure the child does not get hurt, and to the extent that the child is small enough and the adult strong enough to be able to handle him without harmfully straining himself. Depending on circumstances, these may include holding and tossing, or dropping partway to the ground, pretending to throw away, various kinds of swinging, catching the child as he jumps from a low elevation or from a swing, holding one hand and one foot in each hand and swinging him beneath your legs with his eyes closed to an unknown destination, carrying on shoulders or piggyback or on all fours, and many others of the child's or of your devising.

In the water the adult can help the child learn to swim, sometimes having him swim to him and catching him up, and also he can cup his hands to facilitate the child's climbing up and then toss him or cause him to dive, or, when he gets good at it, tossing him over his head to dive in back, always being careful not to scare him. Many kinds of water games can be devised, with or without the help of floats or balls or other equipment. Land games outdoors and games in the house are good to share, though preferably ones of a non-competitive nature, or at least ones in which partnership sharing is more important than competition. Even competitive games of skill, like tennis and badminton, can be converted into a cooperative form by seeing how many times consecutively the players can help each other at normal range to get the ball over the net, and trying each time to do better than the previous records they have made that day. Another good game is to take a large, light, inflated ball and toss it above a group of players to see how many times they can help each other to keep hitting it up into the air without letting it touch the ground, and without any player hitting it twice in a row or holding it. It should be possible to devise many more cooperative games.

In all activities, except the group ones, occasions arise when it is natural to express affection, either by holding close or by kissing, or both, and the impulse should not be inhibited if the adult sincerely feels affectionate and if the child welcomes it or, better yet, returns it. Sharing affection is one of the main aids to the development of genuine love, and it should not be blocked off if sincere. Our restrictive rules against it are like the rules in a society that believed catching fish to be the supreme purpose of life, that had temples for worship of the art of fishing, but a deep-rooted tradition that nobody might go near any body of water. Even so, some people would catch fish from subterranean channels through cracks in the earth, and some would come by them mysteriously.

To be sure, arousing affection between the sexes, even when one of the participants is a young child, is dangerous in a society such as ours, dominated by lust and egocentricity, but it is powerful, and we need all the legitimate power we can get to promote the highest good. Electricity is also powerful and dangerous, but we do not cease to use it. We merely take precautions that it be used properly. It is of the utmost importance that the child learn to deal with affection properly outside his immediate family before he reaches his teens and the precautions are removed. A space traveler from outside the solar system would be amazed that we should expect to get good results within our present traditions, keeping the children innocent (that is, ignorant and inexperienced) of the genuine love that counts most in life until they are consumed with lust, and then sending them out among other teenagers similarly ignorant to find out for themselves. If we expected them to learn mathematics that way how far would they get? Moreover, in the absence of love, lust is inevitable, and once lust has arisen, love becomes very difficult.

Though it is possible to transform the relationship between most parents and their children into one of genuine love, they do not in most cases at present have that kind of relationship, as the results abundantly prove, and calling it so does not make it so. The greatest obstacle to getting something of outstanding value is to believe that you already have it when you do not. You will lack the energy to make the supreme effort required to achieve it. That is one of the reasons why it usually requires someone outside the immediate family to have a fresh approach and get it started, unless the family previously has had that kind of help, or genuine love has come to them in some other way unusual so far in our society. Lt is safer to assume it is not there and do everything possible to develop it, and among the aids is the natural expression of affection before it is contaminated by lust. It is also of the utmost importance to realize that genuine love can develop and rise to a very high level when the most intimate form of sexual intercourse is not involved.

In addition to reading, gymnastics, participation in games, and expressions of affection, the adult needs to have a genuine interest in the child and all that affects him: his parents, his other relatives and friends, his school work, his hobbies, his fancies, and his ambitions; and to help him where he can, especially in developing better attitudes and better personal relations. With genuine love beginning, all these things come naturally and with joy in the doing. If the child is especially attached to some television programs, it may be valuable to share them with him, though it is important to explain that most such programs are based on the false assumptions of our society: that you must get ahead by pushing the other fellow down, by outsmarting him, that antagonistic feelings are a necessary part of life, that joy comes from acquiring gorgeous things. (These assumptions are repeated endlessly in all the communication media until both children and adults are hypnotized into believing them.) Sometimes it may be possible to play in the snow or skate on the ice (or in a roller rink). And it may in some cases be possible to draw or paint pictures together, do crafts, or sing together or play musical instruments, or dance.

After the adult has become well enough known in the family to be thoroughly trusted, it is helpful to take the child occasionally to fairs or other types of entertainment, or even better for walks in the country or along the shore, where the two can learn to enjoy together the beauty of the running brook, the shades of green and shadows on the hillside, the distant views, and wild animals, or the shells and other life on the beach or rocky crag, or the minerals and the rocks (perhaps with fossils), if such things are possible to reach; or to go with the family on vacation outings to help point out and explain these things. The kind of relationship described by Rachel Carson with her nephew in *The Sense of Wonder* is what is meant here. And finally, when there are quiet opportunities it is most important to talk with the child about what counts most in life and the nature of reality, both seen and unseen, so that understanding and trust, as well as affection, may grow.

All these things will be much easier to do if the adult has the parents' understanding and cooperation and that of other close members of the family. It will be easier for them to point out to the child the adult's being close to reality, and to explain that his outgoing advances are due to his receptivity to the child and his genuine interest in his long-run happiness and welfare, so that the child can begin to value him for these qualities, and not value people, like his relatives, mainly because they are *his* or because they give him things. Genuine love must begin with admiration and understanding of goodness (which the child helps the receptive adult to qualify for), as well as with the expression of affection, and the child needs to reciprocate toward the adult if the love is to build up to any magnitude and really benefit the child. Once the child's capacity for genuine love has really begun to take hold, it will spill over onto the parents and other relatives and then out to other people, and they will share in real, lasting joy far more than could otherwise be possible. It will show in many ways, such as the child doing his chores for the joy of helping those he loves, not as duties, and his looking around for more. He can do this even when he is still subject to coercion, for as Jesus said: "And whosoever shall compel thee to go a mile, go with him twain." That is, love can take over the initiative. An experience of genuine love that has gone as far as this can guide the young person successfully through the problems of the teen ages. It will make him so much more attractive that many more associates will be drawn to him, and he will have many real friends. He will enjoy being able to show the more receptive ones what real love is, and the one who is most receptive he (or she) can marry.

If the parents and other relatives do not help in this way, the adult will have to try to explain it himself, which is, of course, much more difficult and less convincing. In this connection, which is of such vital importance for the welfare of the child, those who merely do not interfere because of neglect of the child are sometimes actually better for him than ones who are overly suspicious and misunderstanding (usually because of egocentric possessiveness) and therefore over-protective. The adult may sometimes get through to the child under these circumstances, but it is very much less likely. There are really very few problem children at this stage, mostly just problem parents, but when the children reach their teens without having experienced real love, they can themselves become very serious problems, as is becoming more and more openly evident. Another pitfall is the child in a poor family who is always demanding candy or other treats, or the already selfish child who sees the adult merely as someone whom he can use. It requires great ingenuity and patience to get around these and develop appreciation of more valuable things and better attitudes. There may not be time or opportunity to do it successfully, at least not without all the help possible. But at the other end of the spectrum there are a few children who are just naturally more receptive, who will come through even under the most adverse circumstances.

There are many ways the child can do his part and grow in character by returning the love and attention bestowed upon him by the adult. Usually it is assumed that all he can do is to be affectionate and make little things for him or pick out little gifts to give him or do little services and express good feeling in words and smiles. These are fine, and they can grow to be more and more meaningful. But if the child knows that what will make the adult happiest is success in contributing to the child's own long-run welfare and happiness, he will try his hardest to do those things which the adult has learned from experience will lead to that result. Especially will he try to develop better attitudes leading toward real love for his parents, his siblings and other relatives, his schoolmates and friends, and even all others, as well as toward the adult who specially loves him and is trying to show him how to develop these attitudes. Honesty and fairness in play, and later in more serious things, are basic requirements. More interest and concern in the happiness of the other participants in a game than in winning, along with enthusiasm for improving one's own capacities, are the essence of good sportsmanship. In contrast, showing favoritism for some particular friends in return for favoritism given back is a false basis for friendships. Doing good work at home and at school, as also later in business or other adult occupations, should not be merely to get ahead competitively or to please some person or persons and make them like you. It should be propelled by the satisfaction of developing your own understanding and capacities to be helpful, the joy of rendering services that are helpful, and the joy of contributing to the happiness of the persons you are in contact with, and eventually even of unknown persons far away. These are the things that lead to real success and happiness.

One of the most natural places to learn to experience genuine love should be in a church Sunday School, but there the traditional emphasis is so strong on remote theory and so much against actual experience of the reality that it seldom can be introduced there. The girls and boys would need to be separated and the classes would have to be kept small, not more than four or five at a time, and the teacher, while reading, would need to hold the children or sit close to them, with an arm around them, in rotation. It would be necessary first, of course, to explain the program to the parents and get their permission, and then the teacher would need to spend at least a couple of hours each week with each child in the home (late afternoons, evenings, or holidays). Some senior citizens of both sexes and other non-working ladies should be able to give their time for this, and if they find out the joy it can bring, will be eager to do so.

A second kind of opportunity in our society for forming a relationship that can be improved and made to be really meaningful personally can sometimes arise between an adult and a teenage adolescent. This kind of opportunity is usually very much more difficult to bring into being and to make fruitful, because as soon as a child reaches teen age he usually becomes much more deeply interested in his peers and less open to adults emotionally, especially to senior citizens. If he has not been reached by that time, it is usually too late. However, the cut-off point is not sharp at age twelve and varies with different individuals. Some children become difficult to reach earlier, and some remain somewhat open longer, and it also depends much on the adult. Some handicapped children may remain open much longer, but handicapped persons are another kind of opportunity that will be discussed later. In some cases an adolescent may be specially inspired by a particular adult intellectually or as a hero figure (or heroine), or develop a "crush" on a teacher or other person of the opposite sex, and be particularly open to that one. If receptivity remains or develops for whatever reason during this stage of life, it may, if handled correctly, provide an opportunity for significant creative development.

Adolescents have frequent contacts with adults outside the family, either as teachers or in other capacities, and in cases where there is an inspiring influence, it usually is because of the adult's intellectual or emotional integrity, or preferably both. It may be because of physical or intellectual courage or skill, inducing admiration and a desire to imitate. It may have an impact on the younger person's whole life, producing interest in a trade or a hobby or even a profession, and sometimes modifying character upward (less often downward). But if there is to be introduced at this stage a new element that will contribute toward raising society to a new level, giving genuine love more influence, there must sometimes be more of an all-round balanced personal relationship, including positive personal emotion that can become very much more effective with sincere expressions of affection supplementing the intellectual inspiration. (It would be unbalanced the other way if taken up without the intellectual enthusiasm.)

Besides the circumstance that most adolescents in their teens are not emotionally open to constructively minded adults, another new factor that makes this kind of relationship difficult to handle constructively is the awareness in the background that it is now possible to divert the previous intimacy between the sexes to full adult expression without physical injury. Experience with pre-teenagers shows that genuine love can be developed to a very high level without thought or expectation of this form of sexual intimacy, and thus it can also be so with later stages, too. In view of the almost universal tendency in world society, past and present, to mistake invalid imitations for genuine love, the indication is strong that even the most enthusiastic expressions of affection be kept free from exploitation in this way. The withholding is a powerful influence toward making the relationship grow into an all-round balanced one that can ripen into genuine love.

All this is also true of premarital relationships among adolescents themselves. Some people feel it is possible to experiment with intimate relations beforehand without serious undesirable psychological effects; but if genuine love is not present, doing that is bound to cause serious damage and make it more difficult ever to reach genuine love, while if it is present, everyone would want to follow a responsible course. Full expression of sex prematurely usually leads to a relationship that is disappointing and disillusioning, interfering with the concept that there is such a thing as genuine love and putting in its place an emphasis on single or mutual self-indulgence. On the other hand, it may sometimes happen that an adult and adolescent, in the kind of constructive relationship recommended here, will want to marry, but if the ages are too discrepant there are usually many considerations that would show it to be undesirable for either or both parties, and so genuine love would rule that out also.

In cases where personal adult-adolescent relationships can become meaningful, most of the same observations apply as to the earlier type of relationship, except for the greater care that needs to be taken, by the participants and by the family of the adolescent, to avoid situations in which the temptations to carry physical intimacy too far and make the relationship lopsided would be too strong. There should be no blanket assumption that a mildly affectionate relationship between a teacher and a student or between any qualified adult and an adolescent is unethical, but for safety's sake it should be developed in the home. There it should not be subjected to undue restraint or interference, but should be encouraged with sympathy and understanding. Of course, a teacher could not develop such a close personal relationship with more than a very few of his students, and in the classroom he would have to be scrupulously careful to avoid any favoritism. Indeed, favoritism of any kind is to be avoided in any situation whenever more than one person of the same status or potential status is present.

Another opportunity for more meaningful relationships could be provided by organizing fellowship groups among high school and college students. The idea would be to start with groups of students who are self-selected because they are especially conscientious, to insure that the program would be successful from the start in doing what it is intended to do. Eligible students could be members of religious organizations such as the Student Christian Association (combined Young Women's and Young Men's Christian Associations), campus divisions of other religious groups, students distinguished by scholastic attainments, and student service leaders. Later, if the program has become so successful that others want to join also, they could be admitted on condition that they live up to standards already set by the original groups. A campus coordinator, consisting of an individual or a staff or parent-teacher committee, assisted by students, could allocate applicants to units of approximately twelve, equally divided between the sexes, on the basis of a questionnaire and an interview. Experimentally they could be guided by two different principles, so far as practicable in accordance with a preference expressed by each student. Some homogeneous units could be selected to have members with similar backgrounds and similar interests, to be as congenial as possible, members who would likely be considered eligible marriage partners. On the other hand, there could be rainbow units made up of members with great diversity. Possibly some individuals could belong to one of each type. Then it could be tested to see which type would work better, and it might be found that both types would be of permanent value. Provision should be made for a short trial period, before the end of which a member not happy in a group could change to another; but change later than the end of the trial period should be strictly avoided, except in extreme cases of emerging incompatibility.

These fellowship units would each have one or more advisors selected from the faculty or community because of a combination of reliable character and sympathetic interest in students, and who would recommend, assist, and participate in their activities and would encourage the group to engage in as many wholesome recreational and service activities as possible, such as luncheon, dinner, or just dessert meetings at members' houses, followed by group singing and instrument playing, dances, or discussion sessions; picnics in the park, in the mountains, or on the beach, with hikes or sports; group attendance at public dances or shows or other public exhibitions; group participation in community improvement, cultural, and welfare projects. There should be times, not infrequently, for serious quiet consideration of subjects such as what really counts in life, with group reading aloud followed by discussion and even prayer or meditation.

The object would be for all the members to get to know each other well in an all-round balanced way while engaging in beneficial activities. Members should feel free to be affectionate with each other, with sensitivity to respect the other person's inclination or lack of inclination for it. But while the group is together there should be no favoritism, continuing exclusiveness, or cliques within the group, nor should there be exclusiveness on the part of individuals toward persons outside the group. Members should be free to develop personal relations with other members or with non-members at other times which do not conflict with group activities. However, in making application to join the program, the individuals should pledge to give the group activities priority over others, except for school obligations, major obligations at home, and serious emergencies. They should also pledge not to play favorites and to keep expression of affection, within the group and also outside it, at moderate levels.

If these specifications are followed, each member of a unit should in time, through happy experiences, know well approximately six representatives of the opposite sex and be able to develop a scale of values for different persons, according to the degree with which they can make long-run effective progress together toward reality. It is not to be expected that they would necessarily marry someone in the group, but they could apply their scale of values to persons within the group and outside it as a guide to making more successful marriages, which would be of great value in improving the level of our social success. It should be far better than our present system of "going steady" with one person, which puts such an artificial premium on that one person that it is most of the time not possible to recognize if he (or she) is utterly unsuitable as a marriage partner. The all-round fellowship program will tend to promote genuine love, whereas the "going steady" with one person tends to lead toward the indulgence of lust in a lopsided way. Also, the fellowship program will offer to many young persons a wider range of meaningful contacts than they would otherwise be able to make without its aid, and introduce them to a wider sphere of interests.

Some groups may want to break up and be reshuffled at the end of a year or two, or they may want to keep going longer, perhaps continuing for many years on an altered basis, with the deepening of some couple relationships and the inclusion of sweethearts and spouses or others who were not formerly members, and with the probable dropping out of some, so that the group would gradually evolve. Its life could be as long as the association continued to have a constructive value. Care should be taken, however, to avoid developing a "We-They" attitude toward outsiders.

Courtship, of course, should be a most propitious stage for developing genuine love, though at present it seldom is because of the overwhelming drive toward the indulgence of lust, due to not beginning the development of the capacity for love previously. To insure that it proceeds in the right direction, it is important to develop it in an all-round way, not basing it only on physical attraction and on some special interest such as dancing, playing some simple, easy musical instrument, working together on some hobby, or even belonging to the same church, unless the church connection includes broadening the interests to sincere and active seeking for Ultimate Reality in all aspects of living. There needs especially to be a foundation of understanding of reality or a consensus on how to work toward it and on the importance of working toward it actively. Love is not genuine unless it provokes a more positive attitude toward other people, especially those closest. For instance, there is not room for fear or antagonism against a rival, for if the other person is better for the beloved than you are, that is what you want. Since it often is not clear who is best, your concern should be that all aspects be known as fully as practicable before a decision is made, and then trust to the judgment of the beloved, without hard feelings, if you lose. Of course, if you are the one making the judgment, it is important to make the decision on fundamentals and not on egocentric motives. Promises or implied commitments should not be factors.

The aim should be to bring out and add to the best in each one, to share and participate so far as you can in real concerns and enjoyments. Reasonable unanimity as to work, house, and children is important, and especially an ability to communicate, trusting the other person with what you really feel, and being open to see the other person's point of view, in order to be able to resolve or not be troubled by disagreements. Frequently in cases of disagreements you cannot depend upon the particular words the other person uses but must look for the element of valid feeling back of the words, for one exists, and you can find it if you go back far enough. If you can develop a well-founded, all-round relationship for a considerable period of time, such as several months of spending a lot of time together, or a few years of sparser contacts, with a rising feeling for the whole person and what he or she stands for, you may be ready for the next step. You need to know the other person well enough to know what he mainly stands for, and to be so enthusiastic about it that you can participate wholeheartedly in supporting it. Also you need to know that he does not have any serious hangups, for they are incompatible with love and need to be reliably eliminated first. To marry a person to reform him (or her) does not work. The rule for proceeding further should be that you are ready when you have the symptoms of genuine love as described above, and in the preceding section of this book, and when the expectation of intimate sexual intercourse is not the outstanding factor in it.

Genuine marriage offers the best opportunities for the continued development of genuine love, with much time together and chances to cooperate in many ways and share many experiences. But conventional marriages usually do not work out that way, because seldom has genuine love been developed beforehand, or an all-round basis for it established. The institution of marriage has been terribly misunderstood and abused. Going before a magistrate and signing a contract, or even going through a church ceremony, does not make a marriage. Nothing but genuine love can do this. Only those who have attained genuine love has God put together so that "they twain shall be one flesh," and "let not man put asunder." For God is Love, not a magistrate or marriage clerk, or even a church official, though the last may claim to be God's representative. That is why divorce from a mechanical or legal imitation of marriage is justified and proper and has been practiced, as Jesus explained revealingly "because you knew so little of the meaning of love" (Phillips translation, Matt. 19:8; Mark 10:5). But if it is a real marriage, based on genuine love, no man could put it asunder. That is the fundamental, basic, or original principle, at least until we reach a still more advanced stage when love in the Kingdom of Heaven is universal, as with the angels, and we do not make a special case of any particular person (Mark 12:25).

If a couple has already entered into the outward form of a marriage, and the relationship has not risen above the level that is normal in our society, they should first of all try hard and sincerely over a period of years to make it into a real marriage, especially if they have children. How difficult this may be will depend on the progress each of the individuals has made toward overcoming his (or her) egocentricities (self-limiting patterns), and on how rigidly the habits have formed of living on the lower levels. It will require them to open out and reveal their inner feelings to each other, trustingly and sincerely, to work persistently to overcome their own self-limiting patterns and to let the spouse and perhaps others help with this; to work together to find the way toward Ultimate Reality and the joy of making progress toward it, and to begin to become aware of the real inner core in the other person, inside the obscuring shell. Sometimes joining "sensitivity groups" will help, if there is a skillful, tactful, positive-oriented leader. Negative attitudes which individuals may harbor against each other, sometimes subconsciously, need to be gotten out and eliminated by removing the causes, or by showing their insubstantiality and the futility of the negative feelings; but it is even more important to develop positive grounds for cooperative effort and improved understanding and feeling, to seek out, develop, and emphasize real values in each person. Another help may be prayer and meditation groups connected with a church. No stone should be left unturned.

If one member of the partnership is unaware of the need to make an effort, the other will need to keep insisting, and if necessary to put on mild pressure, gradually increasing, in the form of withdrawing support for the other's egocentric indulgences (financial support for extravagances, catering to possessiveness, sexual services). At the same time, these measures need to be counteracted by increasing support (appreciation and assistance) for all positive tendencies, and by increasing efforts to overcome one's own deficiencies. Marriage should not be regarded as a safe harbor into which you have brought your partner, so that you no longer need to keep renewing the enticement by remaining personally clean and attractive, considerate, sympathetic, interested, enterprising, and industrious. And especially, there must be no feeling of superiority. If there is any superiority, it is only skin-deep and does not go down into the core. It can be accounted for by the accidents of past experiences, and no one can judge which one has made the best use of such past opportunities and pitfalls as have been his lot. Nevertheless it remains the responsibility of the individual not to make excuses for these past experiences but for the sake of his own welfare, as well as his partner's, to overcome his own deficiencies and develop new capacities.

Moreover, no attempt should be made to hold together a nominal marriage by opposing or resisting the development of other constructively meaningful relationships. Neither spouse owns the other or has "rights" in the other, only more than usual opportunities. Looked at the other way around, neither spouse has obligations to the other to avoid situations in which genuine love may develop or to impede its growth, for that is the fundamental purpose of all life which is not too far off the track to realize it. No long-range promises should be made, or, if made, they should not be considered binding, for it is impossible to see far enough into the future to know that with changed conditions it may not then have become wrong to keep such promises. Relieving the institution of marriage of the burden of a false sense of security will reduce the lethargy that interferes with the making of progress within it. If, with greater internal opportunities actively cultivated, the nominal marriage rises to the level of true marriage, based on genuine love, no subsidiary relationship could threaten it. In such a case, one person can so fully occupy the innermost portion of the heart that the two merge in joyful feeling and understanding, and "become one flesh," and the physical expression of the love between them, exceeding the wildest imaginings in richness and beauty, is but one phase of their all-round relationship. There is nothing left over for the indulgence of lust with anyone, but relationships with other persons can rise to high levels of genuine love, too, and be expressed, among other ways, where appropriate, by the tenderest affection. If, on the other hand, the nominal or "pretend" marriage, even with its special opportunities, does not reach the level of genuine love, it does not retain so much importance that it should be allowed to stand in the way of other possibilities for developing genuine love.

126

Nothing said here, however, should be taken as justifying the indulgence of lust, or fornication, which is intimate sexual intercourse without genuine love. Since genuine love is seldom developed enough in our society to be a controlling influence, fornication is committed at the present time by nearly everybody, and though it may come as a surprise to most people, it is practiced more commonly within nominal marriages than outside them. Wherever it is, it interferes with the development of genuine love. Adultery, which is the dilution or contamination of something very fine (in this case, genuine love), by something inferior, must by the same token be very rare. In our society there is not enough genuine love to dilute, and where it does occur there is no temptation to dilute or contaminate it. Thus adultery could be a danger only in borderline cases, in which genuine love is not yet up to the level of control. In such cases it may be very serious, tending to head off the supreme achievement. Here too, it is more likely to be committed within a nominal marriage than outside it, by performing sexual and other services that indulge egocentricities in order to maintain status, rather than risk unpopularity by pulling toward higher standards within, and not valuing more highly a genuine love relationship that is developing outside. Such servility to a lower order could result in gradual or rapid loss of sexual and other forms of sensitivity, along with the capacity to accomplish real good.

Jesus, in His characteristic way of seeing reality without regard to legalistic or nominal or mechanical distinctions, said: "Whosoever looketh on a woman to lust after her hath committed adultery with her already in his heart." As that is not the kind of statement that anyone else would be likely to make up, it is almost certainly authentic; but one wonders if the original word that he used, presumably in Aramaic, that has been reported and translated as "adultery," may not have been a more general term, including the more common "fornication." The purpose of recognizing these sins is not to justify others in condemning those who commit them, if there are any qualified to cast the first stone (or any stone); Jesus did not do that. The purpose is to make everybody aware that they interfere with the development of genuine love, a tremendous cost (or, if you prefer, a severe punishment built in and automatic). Jesus advised them to quit.

It may be asked; if legal, or ceremonial religious, nominal marriage conveys so little in the form of "rights" or privileges upon the participants, why enter into it at all? Many young people are deciding that it is not worth the complications and the costs. There is, however, little or no chance of developing genuine love without feeling full responsibility and lasting considerateness, and the legalized forms provide an available means of taking care of the minimum of these in the face of unknown contingencies. Making tax, inheritance, and other legal relations definite may be of only minor importance, but provision for the support of children and of the mother when they are young is essential. The marriage contract should have them as its main object.

Though reduction of the world-wide population explosion is most urgent—second in importance only to the need for developing more genuine love—there is a pressing need for more children in homes controlled by genuine love, and in ones where genuine love can be introduced. Such children will be able to help show the way toward reality, with experiences of greater happiness utilizing fewer natural resources, and also cutting down on waste through reduction of human conflicts and human negligence. Thus they can save more than their social costs. It is doubtful if genuine love between adults can be complete without the desire to round it out by sharing responsibility for children when that is possible. The parent-child relationship is an important one for the parents as well as for the child, even though, as previously explained, it is not the only one important for the child. If the child is brought up with real love instead of egocentric indulgence or egocentric domination, he can contribute tremendously to the parents' happiness.

The family is an essential part of a healthy society, and the institution of marriage is an aid to it if the right attitudes are maintained within it. If not, it should not involve so much rigidity that a new relationship cannot be made, capable of exchanging a nominal marriage for one controlled by genuine love. Such conversions would be best for the children, for the reconstituted parental pair, and even if the one who has not been ready to take the step forward is left out—best for that one, too, for it will stir him (or her) out of routine habits and inertia, and require efforts to adjust to the stimulation of new relationships, which will either bring out the overlooked values of the old or will offer a new way to get through, or both. If loyalty to a nominal marriage is not expected, it will not hurt so much when it becomes evident that it is wrong to maintain it. The emphasis needs to be on the development of genuine love instead of on the maintenance of a relationship that does not have it.

In our society, which is dominated by lust instead of by love, it often happens that a husband leaves his wife because he is attracted by a younger woman. Usually neither spouse has known it was possible nor thought it important to develop the capacity for genuine love. The wife may have worked hard keeping up the home and bringing up the children, and may have put up with a lot of ill treatment out of a questionably valid sense of loyalty, and her physical beauty has faded away. On the other hand, she may have been developing the capacity for genuine love, in which case a more fundamental kind of attractiveness would continue to shine through even an aging body. A still immature husband may leave even that kind of person; but if she has developed so far, it would be less likely that he would have failed to catch some of it, and he would be appreciative and able to remain happy in the relationship, with or without other kinds of human contacts that may go along with it legitimately. Of course, the relations may have been the other way around, and the wife may have been the one to go off with an outside infatuation. No matter what stage of development the participants have reached, if the marriage breaks up, all is not lost. Even at the eleventh hour it is still possible for each to begin to learn what genuine love is and to develop a capacity for it, or to continue a development partly begun, and thus find real happiness.

A young girl who is herself immature may fall for a man who comes to her in a still immature condition, such as that referred to above, especially if he has wealth or some other form of prestige, for he will make himself appear as attractive as possible; but she will usually be letting herself in for an adjustment to life that will be difficult to deal with constructively. By then his egocentric shell is usually pretty thick, which makes him also likely to be fooled by a shallow woman. However, there are sometimes possibilities even there. Also, it is wrong to assume that all older men and younger women are in that state. There are even now a few exceptions, and it is to be hoped that in the course of time there will be many more. The individual will then be recognized by a receptive person according to his (or her) own merits.

Adults of all ages, married or unmarried, and even including some adolescents, can prepare themselves for growth in genuine love by participating in adult prayer, study, and fellowship groups. In a few cases these may develop out of adolescent fellowship units, but usually they will form in connection with a church or some other organization with constructive intent. Samples of groups that are more or less like what these should be are described in a book edited and interpreted by John L. Castell called *Spiritual Renewal through Personal Groups.* The ones described are of very diverse make-up and character, but they all seem to have produced stimulating and inspiring results far beyond the most hopeful expectations and imaginings of the participants, and very surprising to outside observers. The two fundamental requirements for success seem to be: (1) loyalty of the members, with regular attendance of the same persons at meetings once a week or once every two weeks, giving the group priority over everything else except emergencies and other special matters of great importance, and faithfulness in carrying out agreed upon preparation, whether reading or study or modification of daily habits; and (2) sincere endeavor on the part of the members to be honest and open and receptive toward each other, expressing frankly what they really believe and deeply feel, so that they may grow gradually to know and trust and eventually love each other. As with adolescent groups, it is generally agreed that there should not be more than about twelve members. Some groups may be strengthened by homogeneity and congeniality, others by diversity of backgrounds, interests, ages, social status, etc., but for the most complete coverage the members should be about equally balanced between the sexes.

Usually to get a group started requires that a leader (sometimes a minister) or two or three persons make a proposal that appeals sufficiently to others to induce them to make serious commitments. Then, when the group gets started well, if it is really to function as a group, the leader or leaders must either withdraw or retire to a level of equality with the others. Final decisions would need to be made not by majority vote but by the Quaker principle of getting a sense of the meeting, showing respect even to a minority of one by seeking a deeper foundation, if necessary, to reach mutual understanding. The planned content of meetings should be decided upon by agreement, but it is suggested that they start promptly at a specified hour with a time of silent prayer or meditation, at first brief, followed by a shared meal, either quietly or with one of the members reading a selection of constructive import, and then a discussion of the reading and of other topics. The purpose of the group should be to get closer to reality, and if this is steadily kept in focus, it will bring with it the joy of closer and closer fellowship.

The members should strive continuously to get rid of dogmatism, of adhesions to prejudice. That is the real meaning of prayer: the opening up of receptivity by relaxing the barriers of the ego. Prayer has been so misunderstood and abused that its mere mention tends to throw many people off the track, but it is such an important process that we cannot afford to neglect it. It is not (as you might suppose from most spoken prayers) a technique for changing reality, or God, of informing Him of what He must be supposed not to know, or to have inadvertently overlooked, of imploring Him to do some good thing that He would not be good enough to do of His own accord, or does not know needs to be done, or of getting Him to do what we ought to be doing ourselves. That is all so contrary to both scientific and religious theory as to discredit the process thoroughly. Prayer is really a technique for changing the one who prays, or someone else who may be affected by it, by helping him to see reality more clearly through relaxing distorted prejudices, and so enabling him to line up with reality more closely and enjoy its benefits. One can, while thinking quietly with oneself, take every thought that comes forward and try to relate it to a center containing the best of truth and understanding that one has acquired from experience and instruction. In that way, one's many and diverse inner selves can gradually become organized into a more constructive whole. That is why it is helpful to start with prayer.

Then it is important to be aware of the tremendous amount that we don't know. Thomas Carlyle used to quote that what we know is a drop, what we don't know is an ocean. We have found out so much since his time that what we know now may be a full bucket, but what we don't know is still an ocean. That is why we cannot afford to be dogmatic, to be unreceptive to ideas or data that run counter to our prejudices. We used to think that solid matter was something especially objective and real, but now we find from analysis of information from submicroscopic impulses that it is mostly empty space, with relatively minute concentrations of energy scattered through it and held together by forces that tend to keep them in place. Nothing seems real but the energy, which seems to act sometimes like tiny particles and sometimes like waves, and we classify it, in the different forms in which it comes, into the electromagnetic spectrum according to the wavelengths which grade continuously from the very long electric radio waves, through heat waves, through the waves of the visible light spectrum, and through ultra-violet and x-rays, etc., to the extremely short cosmic rays. Yet we really do not know what it is or how it is transmitted. It is hard to conceive of particles or corpuscles or even quanta of energy traveling almost instantaneously in radio reports from spacecraft in far portions of the Solar System or, with greater time intervals, from radio or light sources in distant galaxies. We used to postulate an imaginary substance called "ether" to occupy space for the waves to be propagated in, but no one really believes in the ether now. Yet it is through inferences from information transmitted in some such way that we have derived all our knowledge of the very large and the very small entities in our universe.

Another example of our fundamental ignorance is that we really do not know what gravity is, why every particle of matter attracts every other particle. It is the one kind of force that cannot be screened out by any kind of obstruction, as we can screen out light or any other form of radiation or magnetism if we use a heavy enough kind of screen. We can counteract it with other forces, and it can become so diluted in faraway space that it is weaker than the radiation pressures that drive the galaxies apart. The ancients used to call anything they didn't understand a demon, and they could sometimes observe the characteristics or habits of the demon, as we can measure and calculate the strength of gravity. Our term is only a more sophisticated one than "demon." It has been suggested that gravity may be the effect of a force operating in a fourth or higher dimension of space pulling out of shape the lines of force in our better known three dimensions, just as a truck resting on the originally two-dimensional flat surface of ice on a pond may cause a depression that will make a ball rolled across the ice deflect toward it, more if it is nearer it, more if the truck is heavier, and with greater force if the ball is heavier. That analogy is less complete than the general mathematical concept that it may be due to multiple curvatures of space, and the latter can at least provide more accurate calculations of gravity, but the reality back of it is still a mystery.

Even the laws of matter that we are most familiar with and feel most confident about are due to the movements of myriads of sub-atomic bits or waves of energy, and these laws hold because of the statistical certainty of large numbers. Insurance companies have compilations of statistics of the lives and deaths of many millions of people, and although they cannot tell just how long you will live, they know with a high degree of precision just how many of any particular class of persons will die in a particular year. But their calculations may be upset by a new factor, such as a war or a pestilence, or a change in a people's social habits. Similarly, a new idea may galvanize a mob that was previously milling about at random or acting in habitual ways and make it press in a new direction. So one or more factors now unknown may at any time modify the operations of the tiny bits of energy that make up matter and produce utterly surprising results. Indeed, many things that are familiar today would have appeared miraculous one or two hundred years ago. Furthermore, our great discoveries or breakthroughs during this time have all been along certain related lines, all restricted within limited parts of reality, selected from the whole on scientific grounds. If we take a more complete, better balanced view of reality, we may encounter even more momentous breakthroughs.

One more consideration tends to make the taking of a dogmatic stand unjustifiable. Everything we know is conditioned by our means of knowing it. The study of this subject is called epistemology. Sir Arthur Eddington gives a very clear and graphic illustration of this: A fisherman using a net makes repeated hauls and then carefully records all that he has taken in. He comes to two general conclusions: (1) there is nothing in the sea less than two inches long, and (2) all sea life has gills. The first is an epistemological law, due to the mesh of his net. The laws of physical science are of this nature. We may, by changing our methods of observation, modify them, but we shall always be dependent on our means of observation and shall miss whatever they are not capable of revealing. Most of our physical measurements, direct or indirect, are dependent on some form of this radiant energy which we do not fully understand. The laws of matter are more a property of this means of measurement than they are of the reality back of it. The other conclusion reached by the fisherman is more characteristic of biological observations. If we look far enough, we shall find exceptions. We can get at reality through biology in a way different from that of the physical sciences.

Another very important instrument used in making all observations is the human consciousness. It, too, has limitations that cut out awareness of reality, but it is evolving, and along with the subordinate instruments it utilizes, may be expected to keep on discovering more of reality. That its present stage of development is not a static one incapable of improvement is shown by its past progress from more limited stages. We may live in a three-dimensional universe because we have a mind in a three-dimensional stage of consciousness. Single-celled primitive organisms incapable of voluntary movement may be said to have awareness with zero dimensions of space. Primitive creatures capable of intentional moving about, from the Flagellates on up, and including perhaps even some of the higher bacteria, have only a one-dimensional awareness.

Snails, for instance, though they live in the same universe we do and go forward and sideways, and up and down, have only an awareness that could be plotted along a single line consisting of a sequence, perhaps from barren and dry to moist to something eatable and back again. Plants and other sessile creatures may have reverted largely to the lower level. Animals that look around and move more freely, choosing between alternatives that they can have in mind at the same time, live in a two-dimensional consciousness, for without stereoscopic vision they do not see depth, do not see the third dimension. From monkeys on, the anthropoid Primates have had the ability to see the third dimension directly. Eagles, dogs, and other higher animals have learned, of course, to make allowances for it, through habits built up from trial and error, though they probably do not realize that is what they are doing. We who are aware of three dimensions of space make allowances also for the effects of time, though we cannot visualize it as directly or immediately.

It is possible that we really live in a multidimensional universe in which the effects of all movements in the higher dimensions are consolidated in the impression of time. Mathematicians have no difficulty in dealing with a multidimensional universe and suspect that there must be something about it that is real. For instance, their calculations of gravity as due to curvatures in many dimensions, according to Einstein's principles, give more accurate results than Newton's law does. Edwin Abbott gives an amusing imaginative description, in his *Flatland, by A Square,* of what life might be like in a (nearly) two-dimensional universe, and of how bigoted the Flatlanders could be about any suggestions of a third dimension. P. D. Ouspensky, in his *Tertium Organum,* gives an illustration of how higher dimensions may be related to time. He imagines a people living in a two-dimensional flatland and observing a wheel in three dimensions intersecting their plane. The wheel has spokes of different colors in regular sequence, and as it rotates slowly the observers become familiar with the sequence so that at one time when a red spoke is in their plane they can say it is "present," while a yellow spoke that has moved out of their plane they can say is "past," and they can predict that a blue spoke which is next in sequence will in time appear and call it "future."

Enlargement of consciousness to retrieve some of what has been lost through the passage of time would, of course, have very exciting possibilities. As yet evidence for precognition has not been weighty enough to be conclusive, but if it should be real, the vision toward the future would necessarily have to fade off or become hazy, since many things in the future are not yet determined. When we get below the statistics of large numbers which apply to gross material objects, there is an uncertainty. We cannot tell which atom of a radioactive substance will disintegrate next, or precisely when, just as we cannot tell which individual person or persons in a particular age group will die this year. The human consciousness may be restricted by the rigidities of its egocentric pattern or patterns, built up by experiences in the past, so that it can only respond with reflex actions to events around it; but severe experiences and sometimes even subtle ones may occasionally break through a shell and bring out something new; and when egocentricity has been reduced and genuine love developed, there can be freedom of the will. We can of course predict occurrences that are highly probable, and they can be fairly definite in precognitive vision. The most plausible explanation of possible cases of precognition is that to some consciousnesses the present is not just a point or line or plane separating the past from the future, but a wider, or widening, slit through which can be seen simultaneously the passage of events a little way into the past and a little way into the future.

Direct awareness of more than three dimensions of space would also raise many more possibilities, especially if space is curved. It might be possible to take shortcuts to extremely distant places in the universe that are utterly inaccessible in a world of only three dimensions. It might be possible to reach places more quickly on earth, or to get around barriers, though that would not be so important. It would mean a general softening up of limitations. Most important of all, of course, would be the softening up of limitations within consciousness itself, the breaking down of barriers, or buffers, and the dissolving away of prejudices. That is also the means of making progress in the evolution of consciousness.

Another question is the continuity of consciousness after death. We cannot get any direct evidence for or against it, at least at our present level of awareness, but we can imagine how it could be. Our bodies may be somewhat like a radio or television receiving set, which may wear out, or someone may take an axe and smash it, but the program goes on just the same. There may be defects in the material utilized, like a knot in the wood of a cabinet, or defects may develop later on. Abuse can multiply the defects. Since we are not purely mechanical, we are not made all at once and do not remain static, but we start with small beginnings and develop as instruments of expression. We store records of past experiences in the brain. These may all go when the instrument is destroyed, but the feeling attitude and ability to influence another development may continue, and we know not what else. There would have to be an important carryback from the development of the consciousness during its earthly experience. It may be that this ability to influence is able to reenter life in a new form, and it may be attracted to the hereditary make-up of a particular fertilized cell of particular parents by compatability, as an ion in solution is attracted to a place in a growing crystal or an electrode, or both. This is, of course, just an analogy and does not provide any evidence or prove anything, but if we can imagine this kind of possibility, there must be many more, and probably better ones, that we cannot imagine.

Thus, the subject of reincarnation is related. Reincarnation is assumed by nearly all primitive peoples, and though their intuition in this matter may not be of any significance, this concept provides the only really plausible means of seeing individual justice in the universal system. Why should an innocent babe be subjected to crippling injury, maltreatment, or disease? It might be that in a previous existence he developed an attitude that attracted him to a situation where these things would occur. Better yet, they could be purely accidental, but if a lifetime is only one among a long series, bad luck and good luck could average out in the long run, as we have our ups and downs from day to day in ordinary experience. A devastating calamity at one time would not be so momentous if there are many more chances. On the positive side, we are much more apt to learn and make progress if we have many opportunities in many different situations. It is possible that a consciousness may progress and develop just as our physical bodies have evolved throughout the history of life. Since there are probably myriads of other places in our vast universe where life stages are overlapping the stages we have here, there might be only a small chance that a consciousness would express itself here again in the next or any succeeding existence. If we could enlarge our consciousness, we might be able to span some of these transitions. However that might be, we are now entering a stage in which we have an opportunity to make such tremendous progress here toward a new way of living, the Kingdom of Heaven on earth, incomparably better than anything known so far, that we should not let slip this known chance, for in any other situations which we might enter hereafter there is no assurance that we will have so good an opportunity again, at least not for many times. Whether there is any hereafter or not, our course here is clear, and it behooves us not to waste any more of our short lives (young or old) spending time on activities that really do not count, or count against us, before taking the steps needed to develop the capacity for genuine love and entering into the joy of real living here and now.

The usual methods that have been applied to effect an expansion of consciousness have been prayer and meditation or other mystical exercises, or the use of drugs. The use of drugs is bound to produce only illusions, for its means are allied with all the other things that produce habit-forming degeneracy. The other methods may produce illusions too, but they are also known to have produced constructive results when practiced properly. In a book entitled *Cosmic Consciousness* Richard Bucke describes fifty cases of more or less expanded consciousness, some of them very important ones. This is a valuable book in spite of what seems like an overemphasis on accessory criteria, such as a sense of illumination, which may not be necessary accompaniments. Actually these fifty cases are only a small sample compared to the many who have received the "Holy Spirit," with or without illumination, such as St. Peter (Acts 12:7, etc.), and the many who have received real inspiration manifested in other ways. William James in his *Varieties of Religious Experience* concludes, at the end of his chapter on "Mysticism," that states of expanded consciousness illustrate a broad spectrum from very positive to very negative. It seems that the integration of the various selves or "I's" in consciousness, giving a sense of authority, can be uplifting, neutral, or degrading, according to whether the psychological center of gravity is in the direction of reality, on a level with ordinary experience, or below it toward unreality.

Bucke wisely points out that even in the uplifting cases the unusual states of consciousness do not in themselves convey infallibility, as in the examples of Gautama the Buddha, and Paul, for the evidence seems to show that these two, because of their great influence, have done incalculable harm through the ages by encouraging the ascetic movements of their times to mislead man into regarding part or all of his natural heritage as evil, thus interfering with the development of genuine love (see especially his pp. 230-232). It seems possible that Paul could have written the great chapter on love in First Corinthians and other illumined passages while in episodes of cosmic consciousness, which are intermittent, and the rest of his teachings in less elevated states of mind. The religions of India often recommend seeking unusual states of consciousness by various forms of artificial manipulation, hoping for self-advancement in ways more subtle than the self-indulgences of drug users, but still seeking self-advancement, and they may even produce remarkable powers. But unless the elimination of egocentricity (Nirvana) is genuine, the product of genuine love, it cannot be expected to result in a long-run benefit to the individual or to mankind. It seems probable that G.I. Gurdjieff acquired some of his unusual powers and influence on associates in these ways, though he remained very egocentric. Some of the Christian mystics also attempted to take Heaven by storm through practices of extreme austerity, like Juan Yepes (St. John of the Cross), but the benefits of psychological accomplishments so produced may be of only limited value. Assurances of reality, which all these people receive, appear to be colored by their previously held views.

In this discussion, too much emphasis may have been put on the continuity of the individual consciousness. In prayer and meditation and any efforts to enlarge consciousness, the emphasis must be put on the decrease of individual egocentricity and prejudices, the barriers that impede the growth of awareness and receptivity. Certainly the development of the capacity for genuine love is the very best method for expanding consciousness, for with that the barriers enclosing the self melt away so that the individual may merge with another, and then continue to spread out to include all mankind.

A century or two ago electricity was a rather rare and little understood phenomenon. Magicians who went around performing sleight of hand tricks, such as pulling rabbits out of hats, also demonstrated what static electricity could do, to the amazement of audiences. Benjamin Franklin was ingenious in showing—with a kite—that lightning is a form of electricity. Materialists at that time who were familiar with the gross laws of mechanics assumed that in the course of time, when more was known about electricity, it would become possible to explain its apparently contradictory behavior in terms of mechanics, so that it would no longer be an alien item in a fundamentally mechanical world. Now that we have learned so much more about electricity, we have discovered instead that we can explain all of mechanics in terms of electricity and the electromagnetic spectrum, though we still do not understand them fully. Today materialists regard the human consciousness with which they perform their experiments, and the human love that attracts one person to another, as odd phenomena which eventually they will be able to explain in terms of the now recognized not-so-material forces and forms of energy. Yet it may again very well be the other way round—that when we have experienced more of a wider range of reality we shall recognize that genuine love is a still more fundamental level of reality, and that all other phenomena can be explained in terms of it. This you can understand only by experiencing it, not by dissecting it or equating it with lust.

When in the course of discussions rigidities of thought and feelings have become sufficiently relaxed, it may be possible to discuss with objectivity events or episodes that have been called miracles (things to wonder at). Psychosomaticists and Christian Scientists have demonstrated that many bodily processes and functions are influenced or controlled by mental and emotional attitudes. Physicians have long known that the patient's will to live often makes the difference between recovery and death. Resistance to germs, especially initially, may have a lot to do with active or passive attitudes. A tendency toward self-pity, leading to gluttony (consumption of large quantities of fats and starches) as a compensation, or the tensions due to internal conflicts may be the main causes of the processes that produce hardening of the arteries, resulting in heart attacks or strokes or premature ageing. It might even be possible that the growth of cells, either benevolent for bodily development and restoration, or malignant and producing cancers, may be stimulated or reduced by changes in consciousness operating through hormones, or by other processes now known or by ones not yet discovered, somewhat as the control lever in an old-fashioned steam engine sets the valves that determine whether the engine goes forward or backward.

Many episodes of healing contrary to the usual operation of natural processes are reported in the Gospels describing the life of Jesus. Much has been made of these and of similar instances of faith healing throughout the centuries, both before His time and after. They have been relied upon as proof of the authenticity of spiritual teachings; and such proof has been generally required even up through the time of George Fox and the early Quakers in seventeenth-century England, and is still looked for by many today. This has created a strong temptation to manufacture or stretch the evidence, or even in perfect sincerity to be swayed by illusions. Standards of accuracy in writing and reporting were very different in early days from what they are now and yet, with all our care and scruples nowadays, if you happen really to know what took place during some reported events, you are often struck by how far the usual reports are from conveying the actual truth. This gives rise to the temptation not to believe anything. Almost surely the emphasis has been put in the wrong place, and we should look in quite a different direction for authentication. Although Jesus is said to have answered the inquiry of John the Baptist by referring to His healing ministry as well as to His teachings, He emphatically belittled those who sought after signs and wonders, who could not recognize reality by its own characteristics.

Surely genuine love must come first, and only then shall we be able to see clearly what these other things mean. Genuine love may be, or may lead to an expansion of consciousness, revealing possibilities that are not now imaginable. Seeking healing for oneself or the power to heal others is often a form of self-concern or self-aggrandizement. It is necessary to lose the self (ego), to be born again, in order to experience reality. Jesus said: "But rather seek ye first the Kingdom of God; and all these things shall be added unto you." Persons who are severely handicapped, physically or mentally, or are so ill they cannot think of anything else, may not be able themselves to seek for genuine love; but if someone who has the capacity for it comes to them, they may be able to recognize it from the way that person treats them, and their responding to it may effect their cure. Jesus would then say that their faith had healed them.

Recent studies have shown that even the membranes within our cells are dynamic fluid structures in which components can move about. In other words even the more rigid parts are adjustable, according to the forces that control them. We should not be surprised at this, for even the atoms in solid inorganic crystals are moveable and subject to modification by the passage of electrons, by diffusion, by a change in the shape of the body, by a change in temperature, etc. Some higher invertebrates have the capacity to regenerate lost parts, such as arms, legs, claws, tails. It is usually assumed that vertebrates cannot do this because the development of each part requires following a more complex biologic pathway, the earlier stages of which would be interfered with by structures or processes now present. However, we cannot know that there do not exist ways to remove these interferences and alter the forces controlling the cells so that they are free to develop and multiply in accordance with their potentialities, all of which they still retain in their hereditary stores. Thus we can relax our dogmatism and allow the possibility that Jesus restored the withered hand, the lame, the blind, the deaf, as well as the persons with fevers, the epileptic, the lepers, etc. Perhaps the timing would remain as the greatest difficulty, but again we must remember that much about the nature of time is still a great mystery to us.

The virgin birth may be a particular problem for some. Such an occurrence is known scientifically as parthenogensis. It is common among some invertebrates. Cases are known of unfertilized hens producing offspring, even of producing roosters. Although it is true that among mammals it is the males that carry the diverse sexual chromosomes, while among birds it is the females which do so, making it easier for them to produce offspring of both sexes parthenogenetically, yet cases are known of human females carrying an extra male chromosome. Hence we have to recognize that virgin birth is biologically possible. If Jesus' descent were entirely from His mother, it might account in part for His unusual sensitivity. On the other hand, the record is contradictory. If Joseph had no part in Jesus' heredity, there would be no point in Matthew's elaborate tracing of his descent from David. Whether Mary received her inspiration and built up her understanding of genuine love entirely through her relationship with Joseph, or had outside help, it is clear from the record that Joseph was a very remarkably sympathetic and understanding person, especially in the context of his times, and he is certainly deserving of more credit than is usually given him for his part in providing an environment favorable for Jesus' development.

The very scanty record does not tell us how much of Jesus' development was due to parental influences, or whether there were other relatives (besides Elizabeth and John the Baptist) or neighbors who contributed. He acquired his capacities in his pre-teens, for by age twelve he was already exhibiting them. He may not have known Martha and her sister Mary until later. It would be much more excitingly inspiring to know that a good mother and father who had reduced their own egocentricities to a minimum, and had experienced genuine love, could produce a child with Jesus' constructive capacities than it would be to assume that it could only be done through supernatural influence. Jesus was emphatic that the things He did, others would do also, if they attained the understanding He had (John 14:12).

Another problem is the raising from the dead and His own resurrection. These would require an enlarged consciousness and the continuity of consciousness after death. Without an actual experience of these, they can neither be proved nor disproved. The evidence purported to be supplied by spiritualists is so far unconvincing, as it has not yielded any important information that ties in with known truth and cannot be ascertained in other ways. The really important point is that the Kingdom of Heaven can be realized and experienced here and now by following the instructions of Jesus and, by doing so, developing the capacity for genuine love. When this has been done, it will be possible to see more of what there is to reality, of what additional influences may be applied to the material scene (that might make possible walking on water, etc.), and finally to make a continuity of consciousness worth while.

For reading and discussing devotional literature and scriptures meaningfully, so that they may be helpful in directing us toward reality, it is important to translate or paraphrase many familiar words and passages into terminology consistent with scientific usages. Thus we can become freshly aware that they have validity in relation to everyday affairs, as well as ultimate considerations, and so take them more seriously and really do some thinking about them, instead of letting them pass off as pleasant, harmless habits of expression that we do not need to pay much attention to. We often repeat traditionally hymns, anthems, scriptural quotations, prayers, creeds, liturgies, and other customary expressions, vaguely aware that we don't really believe what they seem to say, but hoping that there is some meaning behind them that will have a beneficial effect. We can't make much progress toward reality that way. We must stop saying things we really don't believe. We must stop telling God things He doesn't know and imploring Him to do the good He had neglected, or to set things right, when it is *we* who are refusing to do our part. It is too inefficient to keep going off in the wrong direction, even if we make mental reservations and corrections. We must get on with the business of understanding reality.

For instance, take the favorite and beautiful passage from Second Isaiah:

"Even the youths shall faint and be weary, and the young men shall utterly fall: but they that wait upon the Lord shall renew their strength; they shall run and not be weary; and they shall walk and not faint."

It is customary to read this passage and thrill to its beauty, and not be aware that it means for us to do something to make the happy vision come true. What does it mean "to wait upon the Lord?" (I have seen it quoted: "wait for the Lord!") Does it mean wait in readiness to do His bidding when He tells you something more? Or does it mean get busy now and do what the evidence already furnished you shows you must do to bring about good results? It could be paraphrased: Those who steadfastly follow the directions already given for approaching closer to reality shall renew their strength. It also means, of course, to keep sensitive and frequently correct your course as you receive more enlightenment.

Even the "Lord's Prayer," familiar as it is and as much discussed, needs to be converted into realistic terms so that we can carry its meaning over into our striving for progress:

"Our Father	O great and steadfast, true and good, source of our being and Fundamental Reality of the Universe,
Who art in heaven,	fully discernible only when we are conditioned by genuine love to know heavenly paradise,

148

Hallowed be thy name.

we bow in awe before Thy Wonders (seen and not yet seen).

Thy kingdom come,

We long to experience the coming of Thy Kingdom,

Thy will be done on earth,

in which genuine love has the controlling influence among all people,

as it is in heaven.

not merely for a few who have so far reached the heavenly state.

Give us this day our daily bread,

We will open ourselves out daily to receive the bread of the coming day (more awareness of reality), instead of devoting all or most of our time and efforts to maintaining the delusions of past and present egocentric practices.

And forgive us our debts, as we forgive our debtors,

We realize that as we cease to take for personal affronts the lack of receptivity and the other self-limiting actions of unenlightened persons, we shall grow out of negative emotions ourselves.

And lead us not into temptation but deliver us from evil,

We shall not see any sense in self-indulgences or in acting negatively or meaninglessly, and so we shall not be the cause of or suffer from the consequences of actions out of harmony with the universe,

For thine is the kingdom, and the power, and the glory, for ever."

for all control and all strength and all glory consists always in lining up with the real (seen and unseen) universe.

Many other examples could be given. The paraphrases usually need to be more lengthy in order to express clearly the applicability of the passages to present understanding. After the first conversion of the words of hymns, anthems, and other poetic writings, or writings with condensed meaning, into this form, a further step would be to find new words, new similes to get the original and evolved meanings again into metrical and condensed forms that would make them useful for hymns, anthems, memory reminders, and prayers. To do this the paraphrasing would have to be still more liberal, but any device would be desirable that would catch the essence of the original meaning and its relation to reality and render it in attractive form. It would be a beneficial exercise for members of prayer, study, and fellowship groups to experiment with and then later make a regular practice of writing these paraphrases. Also, they could write summaries of chapters or sections of devotional literature they have read, or of studies they have made, and these could be written in both religious language and in realistic equivalents. And, of course, they could also compose wholly new productions.

Another very important field for discussion in the groups is social concerns, leading, it is hoped, to the formation and support of practical projects for human betterment. Intellectual consideration needs to be followed by specific applications. Either stage alone is barren without the other. Good intentions or good feelings, if allowed to evaporate without producing any constructive result, are weakening to those who indulge in them. On the other hand, hasty actions without careful thinking out of the situation or problem often do more harm than good.

A book helpful in laying the foundation for social reform is John Macmurray's *Reason and Emotion*. It is especially good in making clear that feelings as well as thoughts can be either rational or irrational, according to whether they are appropriate to the situation or not; that chastity is emotional sincerity, not dependent upon conformity to external rules but upon expressing a deep inner sincerity that is proof against fooling oneself as well as against fooling others; and that all our institutions, including the church, need to find real maturity. If all the religions of the world would recognize with Macmurray and with the anthropologists that the function of religion is to promote communion and true fellowship within the community, eventually spreading out to all mankind, and would begin to question the validity of any of their practices or concepts that interfere with this function or that do not contribute toward it, they would all begin to approach closer to each other and to reality. The joy of genuine fellowship would spill over into generosity for recognizing validities in the systems of other peoples, for recognizing that reality is available to all peoples throughout the universe, and that some have been more successful in approaching certain aspects of it, while others have been more successful in approaching other aspects. Members of each would hang on less tenaciously to their own special peculiarities, especially ones which turn out to be inconsistent with reality.

If all Christian churches would put less emphasis on traditional forms and more emphasis on the teaching and practice of Jesus, centering on the development of genuine love in personal relations, each would change so much that the differences between sects would become minor. The brotherhood of men would not be theoretical but experienced. Some people might for a time be more comfortable under the types of church organization of their custom and choosing, ranging from very liberal to very authoritarian, so that we might still have, for instance, a Congregational Christian Church of Reality, a Baptist Christian Church of Reality, an Episcopal Christian Church of Reality, and a Roman Catholic

Christian Church of Reality. We might even have a Christian Science Church of Reality, a Mormon Church of Reality, a Hebraic Synagogue of Reality, a Mohammedan Mosque of Reality, a Buddhist Temple of Reality, a Taoist Temple of Reality, a Voodoo Assembly of Reality, etc.

Eventually many of these differences would be dropped. As they would all approach closer to reality, it would become easier to integrate with the part of reality dealt with by science. Paraphrasing their expressions into terminology consistent with science will help. Science also will need to become more liberal and recognize the aspects of reality that are not amenable to its usual methods of investigation, more liberal in realizing that the ability to control nature is not so important as it is for us to conform to the whole of reality.

The foregoing may serve as an illustration of how to bridge gaps and reduce conflicts, such as the gap or lack of understanding between science and religion, the factors separating the different religions (and the sects within them), gaps between liberals and conservatives in religion, in economics, in politics, between labor and management, between generations, sexes, races, nationalities, and other interest groups. The way to lessen conflicts is not to look the situation over, decide which side is right, and then go in to fight for that side. In any large controversy where there are many sincere and conscientious people on all sides there are bound to be elements of truth on which each person bases his position. Even in small controversies there is something valid somewhere back of each aim and view. Others will be seeing the merits of the other side, or sides, and will be going in to support them. If one side is downed by a superior force or more expert persuasion, some of the truth will be downed with it, and it will be coming up again later.

The really helpful thing to do is to identify each of

the valid elements on all sides and creatively integrate them, for with all the valid elements taken into account a solution can be found that is better for all than the goal of any one side. Nearly always much more can be gained by cooperating than by fighting. In the long run the fair solution will be better even for those who might have won. But to seek for and find such a solution and convince all sides of its value requires more patience than can usually be found, except in one who has himself experienced the reality of genuine love. Only he has the equilibrium to be objectively impartial and the persistence to keep at it. The purpose of social concern of any prayer-study-and-fellowship group, or religious social action committee, should be to raise the level of controversy, to bring out all the elements of truth and work on their integration. It is especially important to examine diligently, sympathetically, and understandingly the sides that seem most wrong. It is not enough to take their own statements of the case and criticize or pick holes in them. They often do a poor job in presentation. It is necessary to find the really valid meaning that they are trying to express, and then see how it fits in with the rest of the problem.

Times will come when action is required. When an election day arrives, each individual will have to decide according to whatever light, usually incomplete, he has been able to get on the subject. Some individuals, or the group as a whole, may feel that an issue or a candidate is important enough to warrant the expenditure beforehand of time, energy, or money in an effort to influence others. Even in doing that, however, the sincere individual should try not to exaggerate, not to overstate the merits of the side he has taken temporarily during the campaign, nor to hold back full admission of values on the other side or sides, and then, when the campaign or time for action is over, to go back to cultivating an impartial openness toward valid truth on all sides. It is not unlikely that a person doing this will be able to exert an even stronger influence during times of action, and his influence will be more often constructive.

There are many other forms of action that a group or some of the individuals within it may take, but no person or group should feel obligated to do all the good things that need doing, only those for which he, she, or they are most fitted. Everyone should be exerting a really substantial effort on one or more constructive projects besides a service commitment to make a living, such as: enlarging one's own understanding of reality, and that of others; offering personal encouragement and inspiration to help others make progress beyond present limitations; spreading comfort and joy; helping the handicapped and needy; and working for community improvement in one or more ways. Goal-oriented cooperation is an important requirement for the development of genuine fellowship.

The reason that conflicts and problems are increasing in numbers and severity, as explained above, is that we are violating the basic principle of evolutionary development of needing to maintain an all-round balance of capacities, for we are grossly deficient in our capacity for genuine love, and so we miss real happiness in life and tend to blame others for it. We blame our parents and teachers if we are children, saying they do not understand us, or the social establishment if we are young adults; if we are parents we blame our children for not behaving properly; if we are married we blame our spouses; if we are laborers we blame management; if we are managers or capitalists we blame the big bad unions; if we are small businessmen or farmers we blame the politicians; if we are indigents we blame the government; and if we are politicians we blame the other party or whatever element the majority of voters are against, or we blame foreigners, for foreigners have no votes. But always the main cause of our dissatisfaction is within ourselves, our lack of joy-bringing love. Therefore it follows that our most constructive contribution toward solving conflict problems and reducing the waste of human and natural resources is to seek ways and means to develop more genuine love in as many ways and situations as possible. Some of these ways and situations have been outlined here.

For an adult of any age who has begun to overcome his egocentricities (who is "poor in spirit") there are at least four classes of situations in which he may find genuine love. As already explained, he may seek to have a really creative relation with a young child, in normal cases most effectively with one of the opposite sex. Unless he has made progress in overcoming his own egocentricities, he will merely try to please the child, to induce him to like him, and so accomplish little or no good and fail to experience genuine love. He may even do harm by exploiting. But if he is properly prepared and qualified, this is the most often available kind of opportunity and one with a high probability of success, as recommended by Jesus.

The second class of opportunities is in joining a prayer, study, and fellowship group—getting to know well, then trust, then love the other members. If such a group is not already available in a church or other favorable environment, he can agitate to get one started. Here again, success depends upon the members getting beyond their egocentricities.

The third class of opportunities, though rare at present, should become more common: getting to know someone who has already experienced genuine love. The egocentric will not be able to recognize such a person, preferring other egocentrics who appear to him more glamorous; but one who has made progress will be receptive.

The fourth class is probably the most difficult,

though some should be able to win through by this route. Two persons who have each begun to make progress may help each other to it, as explained in the discussion of courtship, recognizing that even with friendliness and sympathetic understanding for all persons, a particular relationship cannot rise through mutual build-up to reach the lasting joy of entrance into the Kingdom of Heaven unless each becomes qualified by overcoming self-indulgent hang-ups, and gets to know the other person well enough to know that his (or her) main interest in life is broad enough and fine enough to be worthy of enthusiastic, wholehearted support.

Handicapped persons pose special difficulties but also offer special opportunities. If they are full of self-pity and rebellious and bitter because of their deprivations, they may be hard to reach, and only someone who has already known genuine love may be able to do so. That is why uninformed persons, especially in early times, expected them to be witches, dominated by negative feelings. We still use such words as "stupid" and "sinister" (the latter meaning merely left-handed). Often the social outcasts took up the challenge and behaved as expected, or they sought fellowship with each other, and sometimes found it, as in the coven (a form of secret medieval assembly of "witches," limited to twelve members, who practiced a holdover of primitive religious group activities). But now that most kinds of handicapped persons are treated somewhat more reasonably and they do not have so many unnecessary added burdens imposed upon them, they are often not so hard to reach and in many cases are especially receptive to kindnesses shown them. Their courage and accomplishments in overcoming their difficulties, or in living with them and compensating by developing capacities in other ways and positive personal attitudes may inspire admiration, even sometimes to the extent that the handicap may become to others a symbol of endearment. They may do more than solve the problem of establishing equality with outwardly "normal" persons. Nevertheless it will often happen that others with comparable handicaps will be the ones best able to understand and sympathize and help. In part, at least, because of the patience and creative perceptiveness acquired in overcoming her own handicap, Anne Sullivan was able to rescue Helen Keller, deprived in infancy of sight and hearing, from the generally adjudged hopeless condition of a blind "deaf and dumb" person, so that she might become later a speaker and writer of books, whose personal achievement has been an inspiration to millions.

There are many different kinds and degrees of handicaps. Physical deformities can sometimes be corrected or reduced by surgery or modified by therapy. They can be relegated to secondary consideration by genuine love. Mental retardation, if severe, may require much more personal attention and genuine love to produce any positive response. Even though the retardation is less severe, unless the capacity for genuine love has been first developed elsewhere, it is hard to have a thoroughly sincere feeling of equality, and such a relationship, or one involving two similarly retarded persons, would still not be able to achieve an all-round balance without it. Minority racial and ethnic groups are often subjected to artificial handicaps that are hard to overcome, as in the situations of blacks in North America and Orientals in Africa. Personal relations between these and representatives of the majority are sometimes hampered by both sides feeling superior. Sex may also sometimes be considered an example of handicap. In all these cases, so long as either participant feels especially noble for taking part, there cannot be a genuine love relationship.

Regarding homosexuals as handicapped may be partly artificial and partly in accordance with reality. To the extent their relationships are based on lust, they are no worse than most heterosexual relationships. Certainly, also, genuine love can be developed between representatives of the same sex. It is doubtful, however, if fully complementary contributions can be made to produce a complete and balanced whole, with the full potentialities of a personal union; and the inability to produce children for family development, other than acquiring them by adoption, would have to remain another serious handicap. Hence it is wise to seek ways to remove the psychological or physiological blockage to full appreciation of the opposite sex.

Age is another type of handicap. Its impact is not, however, strictly chronological. Some people escape the disadvantages of the age span they are in; others have disadvantages appropriate only for other age spans. As William James pointed out, some people are already old fogies while still in their twenties, trapped in rigidities of habit, with all avenues of progressive development and really enjoyable appreciation of reality closed off. We might add now that a large proportion of teenagers are even more handicapped, not being allowed by their peers to open up to skills and accomplishments that the experience of centuries has shown pay off, after somewhat slow starts, in lasting values. They are, therefore, being confined to monotonous trivialities, or worse, health-destroying indulgences, which would be extremely boring except for the exciting but illusory prospects they have of filling their emotional vacuums through personal associations while sharing such activities.

Younger children are handicapped by their parents not allowing them, at a time when they still have a potential not blocked off, to be open to experiences of genuine love. Young married couples are often handicapped by pressures to supply the physical needs of growing families, so that they think they do not have time to pay attention to the things that really count in life. Mature people in the "prime" of life may be handicapped by being engrossed in the success or the difficulties of business, career, or family development. Senior citizens, even if their health has not been undermined by various forms of self-indulgence at earlier ages, may be left not knowing what to do, or concentrating on pastimes of minor importance. But none of these handicaps need apply, if the opportunities for developing genuine love described above are sought and developed. Some loss of capacities may be expected in old age, but they can be compensated for by a beauty of inner attitude, which will make possible close personal relations in one or more of the four ways enumerated above that are applicable all through this stage, so that this can be the happiest time of life for those who have not found genuine love earlier, and also for those who have, for there is no limit to the continued expansion of consciousness and perception of joy which it confers.

With the possible exception of severe mental retardation, the most serious, as well as the most common type of handicap is imprisonment in a heavy, egocentric, self-limiting shell. If those who have any other kind of handicap can avoid having this one, too, they will be better off and happier than those supposedly normal persons who are afflicted with it. They will be open to the development of genuine love, which can relegate their handicap to a secondary role. Unfortunately, handicaps often come in combinations, and then it is hard to recognize which has the most damaging effect. But this one can be removed and leave the others reduced to their true proportions and subject to further subordination to growing positive capacities.

Perhaps it will help now to list the situations that have been brought up for attention, in which genuine love may be successfully sought:

(1) In a young child-adult relation;
(2) In an adolescent-adult relation;
(3) In student fellowship units;
(4) In courtship;
(5) In marriage;
(6) In adult prayer, study, and fellowship groups;
(7) In the adult end of an adult-child relation;
(8) With someone who already knows genuine love;
(9) With another adult who, like yourself, is seeking to become lovable by overcoming egocentricities and approaching reality;
(10) With handicapped persons.

It is so easy to keep right on in the same old routine habits, letting opportunities slip by, and not going out to seek them, to promote them, and to remove the obstacles that hinder their becoming available. Inertia is *The Evil* that Gerald Heard identifies as primarily what we pray to be delivered from in the final goal passage of the "Lord's Prayer" (see *The Creed of Christ,* Chapter 6). We are absorbed by our successes or hopes of successes in our competitive society of conventional inadequacies, or by trivial amusements, or we are overwhelmed by problems and difficulties, so we can give little attention to what is most important. In times of political, economic, and personal quiet it is business as usual; and in times of severe turmoil, which must needs come, we are too distracted by immediate events to think of anything else. And so we keep supporting the system that leads to disasters and personal decline, to wars, economic strife, crime, waste, pollution, boredom, suffering; and we keep putting off taking the steps that can begin to lead toward much better experiences, more in accord with reality and genuine lasting happiness.

Of the three levels of morality our society is rapidly descending to the lowest. Sex relations are being regarded more and more as primarily for the free and intentionally egocentric indulgence of lust. Formerly, people were kept largely to a middle level of abstinence or restricted practice by the fear of hell or of pregnancy or of social condemnation, or by the hope of individual salvation and heaven in the hereafter, or to cater to the possessiveness and indulgence of a spouse and so maintain status in the family, all essentially egocentric motives, though some more subtle and disguised. Now few people take seriously the idea of hell hereafter, and few are aware of the imminence of an egocentric personal or community hell right here. There are enough doubts about a connection with individual salvation to weaken the resistance to sex drives. Medical techniques and economic reforms have reduced the problems of pregnancy and family dependence to minor proportions. Hence social condemnation also is relaxing. The middle level has become hopelessly unstable. Social conservatives see little that can be done to shore it up, and so can only maintain their peace of mind by looking away. It never did produce the state of general happiness and welfare that it was expected to, and it is now becoming clear that it never could. Its mechanical rules were too inaccurate to produce the desirable results that really can be attained. The solution is not to descend to the lower morality, nor to try to retain the unstable middle level, but to win through to a higher one.

The power of sexual attraction must be directed toward building up better attitudes, instead of trying to suppress it and then inevitably allowing it to break through into degeneracy. A few people at first, and hopefully more and more, can discover that expressing affection more freely to those deserving of it (who really show conscientious, non-egocentric behavior), but keeping in reserve the full expression of sexual intimacy until after a broad base has been established for the growth of genuine love, and until after the love itself has thus been stimulated to grow into the controlling influence, will lead to results far more wonderful than anything previously experienced or imagined. The ego will be lost, at first within the partnership, and later in outreach to the whole community. He who would save his life must lose it, for the sake of what Jesus stood for. Then love will make right actions certain without the need for mechanical rules. If only a tiny part of our population, a few hundreds in the nation, reach this level, they can exert an influence far out of proportion to their numbers and reverse our adverse social trends, reducing the severity of conflicts in all areas, and raising the level of well-being for all. Eventually many more would be encouraged to adopt this standard, too. In this way our psychological all-round balance can be restored and we can get back on the main line of evolutionary development in its progress toward Ultimate Reality.

Although some of the uplifting thoughts incorporated above have been said many times, the new idea here is that evidence from other fields shows we must now really take them seriously. We cannot afford to wait, to drift along with old habits and halfway measures. That way rapid deterioration threatens us. We must turn to more effective ways to promote real progress. The main point of this book is that the valid truths of very diverse disciplines are interrelated, can be fitted together, and that solutions of major problems and increase of well-being and happiness depend upon awareness of the reality that runs through them all: the history of life, the findings of psychology, the teachings of Jesus, and personal experiences of genuine love with children and others.

Recommended Readings

(Citations and comments on books to read to children are given on pp. 104 to 109. In many cases other books by the same authors are also significant.)

Abbott, Edwin A.: *Flatland, by A Square.* New Edition, Little, Brown, and Co., Boston, 1941, 155 pp.

Berrill, N.J.: *The Origin of Vertebrates.* Oxford, 1955, 257 pp.

Buber, Martin: *I and Thou.* Early English Edition, T. & T. Clark, Edinburgh, 1937, 120 pp.; Second Edition, Scribner, N.Y., 1958, 137 pp.: New Translation, Scribner, N.Y., 1970, 185 pp.

Bucke, Richard M.: *Cosmic Consciousness.* First Edition, 1901; Fourth Edition corrected and re-set, Dutton, N.Y., 1923, 384 pp.

Casteel, John L. (Ed.): *Spiritual Renewal through Personal Groups.* Association Press, N.Y., 1957, 220 pp.

Darwin, Charles: *The Origin of Species.* (Many editions.) Especially important are Darwin's own introduction and Chapters 3, 4, and 14 in unabridged editions. It is amazing how many people discuss this influential and still very significant book who have never read it.

Drummond, Henry: *The Greatest Thing in the World.* (Many editions.)

Eddington, Arthur S.: *The Nature of the Physical World.* Cambridge Univ. Press and Macmillan, N.Y., 1928, 361 pp.

————: *The Philosophy of Physical Science.* Same, 1939, 230 pp.

Fromm, Eric: *The Art of Loving.* Harper & Bros., N.Y., 1956, 133 pp. This book is good in telling what love is not, in showing the falsity of common concepts, and it is good in some of its descriptions of the theory of love; but it is weak in guidance toward the experience of love, and very misleading in ascribing our deficiency of genuine love to competition in an economic system of voluntary agreements. The present undesirable features of that competition are due to the same growing egocentricities that interfere with love, which induce people to resort to falsities and unfairness, and without which the striving to produce better goods and services at lower costs and the rewarding in free markets of greater control over resources to those who are more effective in using them well would be entirely wholesome. Even with these present defects, this system is highly preferable to the only alternatives, which necessarily involve some kind of socialistic control by a dictatorial government with the ultimate sanction of military force, suppressing opposition and making democracy unworkable, thus putting individual freedom and security at the mercy of the ruling element. That would make it even harder to generate real love, though it could still be done, as it has been possible, for instance, even in Franco's Spain and in Communist countries.

Heard, Gerald: From his anthropological and sociological series:
The Ascent of Humanity. Jonathan Cape, London, 1929, 332 pp.
The Social Substance of Religion. George Allen & Unwin, London, 1931, 318 pp.
   The Source of Civilization. Jonathan Cape, London, 1935; Harper & Bros., N.Y., 1937, 431 pp. Especially important are the 66 pages from the top of p. 66 to page 132. (The two points on which elsewhere in the book he takes issue with Darwin are apparently due to misconceptions, and in each case I think Darwin was right.)
   Gabriel and the Creatures. Harper & Bros., N.Y., 1952, 244 pp.; English ed. called *Wishing Well*, Faber & Faber, London, 1953, 198 pp. (See comments in section on children's literature.)
————: From his religious series:
The Creed of Christ. Harper & Bros., N.Y., 1940, 169 pp.
The Code of Christ. Harper & Bros., N.Y., 1941, 168 pp.
A Dialogue in the Desert. Harper & Bros., N.Y., 1942, 74 pp.
A Preface to Prayer. Harper & Bros., N.Y., 1944, 250 pp. with Bibliography.
The Gospel according to Gamaliel. Harper & Bros., N.Y., 1945, 154 pp.
Howells, William W.: *Mankind in the Making,* revision of *Mankind So Far.* Doubleday, N.Y., 1967, 384 pp.
————: *Evolution of the Genus Homo.* Addison-Wesley, Reading, Mass.,

1973, 188 pp., this book and the series to which it belongs now taken over by the Cummings Publishing Co. of Palo Alto. California.

James, William: *The Varieties of Religious Experience.* Longmans, Green, & Co., N.Y., 1902, 534 pp. This book puts the emphasis where it belongs, on experience instead of on theory. The author concludes (pp. 511-519, 523 bottom to 524 top) that religious experience points to the reality of a larger self, which includes subconscious regions that the ordinary consciousness is not aware of (but it is influenced by them and can open out to them so as to become beneficially aware), and that beyond the larger self may be a reality other than the self, which also influences by incursions and can be benefically opened out to (and may be called God). I would add that the first reality beyond the enlarged self which one needs to become truly aware of through genuine love is another individual, and only after more and more individuals, and eventually all, are regarded in this way can one become fully aware of Ultimate Reality, or God.

Jung, Carl Gustav: *Psychological Types, or The Psychology of Individuation.* English Edition, K. Paul, Trench, Trubner & Co., London, 1926; Pantheon Books, N.Y., 1962, 654 pp.; a revision by R.F.C. Hull of the former translation by H.G.Baynes, Princeton Univ. Press. 1971, 617 pp.

Kelley, Thomas R.: *A Testament of Devotion.* Harper & Bros., N.Y., 1941, 124 pp.

Kropotkin, Petr: *Mutual Aid, a Factor in Evolution.* 1914, many editions, among the latest: Extending Horizons Books, 11 Beacon St., Boston 8, Mass., 1965; N.Y. Univ. Press, 1972, 277 pp.

Kunkel, Fritz, and Roy E. Dickerson: *How Character Develops.* Scribner's, N.Y., 1940, 274 pp.

Kurtén Björn: *Not from the Apes.* Random House, N.Y., 1972, 183 pp.

Leakey, Louis S. B.: *Adam's Ancestors.* Methuen, London, five editions, the fourth, 1953, 255 pp., completely rewritten. Although now out of date, these editions were the first to suggest a more clarifying explanation.

Leakey, Mary: *Olduvai Gorge,* Vol. 3. Cambridge Univ. Press, 1971, 306 pp. quarto. A magnificent example of a primary research report.

Lévy-Bruhl, Lucien: *How Natives Think.* French original 1910; G. Allen & Unwin, London, 1926, 392 pp.; Washington Square Press, N.Y., 1966, 355 pp.

————: *Primitive Mentality.* G. Allen & Unwin, 1923, Beacon Press, Boston, 1966, 458 pp. A sequel to the preceding.

————: *The "Soul" of the Primitive.* G. Allen & Unwin, 1928, 351 pp.: Praeger, N.Y., 1966.

————: *Primitives and the Supernatural.* E. P. Dutton & Co., N.Y., 1935, 405 pp.: Xerox reproduced, 1970.

Lewis, C.S.: *The Screwtape Letters.* Macmillan, N.Y., 1943, 160 pp.; with new preface and Screwtape toast, 1961, 172 pp.

————: *The Great Divorce.* Macmillan, N.Y., 1946, 128 pp.

————: "The Space Trilogy": *Out of the Silent Planet.* Macmillan, 1944, 160 pp. *Perelandra.* Macmillan, 1944, 222 pp. *That Hideous Strength.* Macmillan, 1946, 382 pp. Obviously, all these allegories have a significant bearing on the problems of our times, besides being entertaining reading. See also his children's books, which adults, understanding the symbolism, will see as important.

MacDonald, George: *Lilith.* 1895; Wm. B. Eerdmans, Grand Rapids, Michigan, 1964, (following *Phantastes*) pp. 183-420. Though in the form of most highly imaginative fantasy, this book, like a prose poem, expresses, as C. S. Lewis points out in his introduction, the essence of heartwarming goodness and appreciation of more fundamental reality. See also his children's books and other writings.

Macmurray, John: *Reason and Emotion.* Faber & Faber, London, 1935; second edition, 1962, 286 pp. A searching exposure of our social structure with implications for its improvement.

Miller, Stanley L., and Leslie E. Orgel: *The Origins of Life on the Earth.* Prentice-Hall, Englewood Cliffs, N.J., 1974, 230 pp. Although parts of this are difficult reading for anyone who has not had an introduction to organic chemistry, the explanations are enough so that the meaning can be dug out.

Oparin, A. I.: *Origin of Life.* Macmillan, N.Y., 1938; Dover, N.Y., 1953, 270 pp.; new translation, Oliver and Boyd, Edinburgh and London, 1957, 495 pp.; *Genesis and Evolutionary Development of Life,* new translation, Academic Press, N.Y., 1968, 203 pp. This is the classic work on the subject. The later and bigger translations are not necessarily better than the 1938 and 1953 editions, according to Miller and Orgel.

Ouspensky, P. D.: *Tertium Organum.* Knopf, N.Y., 1922, 1970, 306 pp.

Romer, Alfred S.: *Vertebrate Paleontology,* 3rd Ed. Univ. of Chicago Press, Chicago and London, 1966, 468 pp., quarto.

Smith, Homer W.: *From Fish to Philosopher.* Little, Brown, & Co., Boston, 1953, 288 pp. A thorough account of the history of the kidney.

Van Dusen, Wilson: *The Natural Depth in Man.* Harper & Row, N.Y., etc., 1972, 197 pp. Though starting with what seems like superficial treatment of surface phenomena, it goes on to tie together deeper aspects of reality, using materials different from those in the present book but turning up some of the same conclusions.

————: *The Presence of Other Worlds, the Findings of Emanuel Swedenborg.* Harper & Row, N.Y., etc. 1974, 240 pp. Chapters 5 and 10 are especially significant. Though there may be some doubts about cosmological meanings, the basic attitudes are certainly valid and important.

Index

Main references and illustrations are indicated by heavy type, **000**; where a subject is discussed but the name not specifically mentioned, it is shown in parentheses (000).

169

Brain, 12, 13, chart stage 6, 23, 28, 33, 34, 36, 39
  nature of, 139
Brain case, 14, chart stages 8, 10 and 13B, 19
Brain to body ratio, 29
Brainwashing by T.V., etc., (70), (112)
Branch lines, 16
  contrast to main line **3**, **chart** (all stages), 35, 42
Brazilian jungle tribes, 53
Bread (daily, or fuel for progress toward the future), 149
Breakthroughs, 135, 138
Bronze age, 60
Brow ridges, 24–25, 28, 29, 35, **(36)**, 37, 42
Bryophyta, chart (left side)
Bryozoa, 14, chart
Buber, Martin, 51, 79, 163
Bucke, Richard, 140–142, 163
Buddist Temple, 152
Buffers, 72, 138
Bull-roarers, 54
Bunyan, John, 109
Burial, 39
Burin, **30**, 31
Burnett, Frances Hodgson, 107
Bushmen, 53
Business, 159

Callousness, 3, 47
Campbell, Bernard, 27, 34
Cancer, 143
Canine fossa, 37, 42
Canine teeth, chart (stages 13A and 19), 25, 26, 42
Cannibalism, 40, 59
Capacity
  for biologic adaptation, 2, 23
  for genuine love, 65, 72–73, 82–83, 85, 86, 89, 102, 107, 113–114, 122, 129, 130, 140, 142, 147, 154
  for human speech, 37
Capitalist-democracy-scientific stage, 63

Capitalists, 154
Career, 159
Caring, 39–40, 43, **76**
Caritas, 76
Carlyle, Thomas, 133
Carnivora (division of mammals), chart, 25
Carnivorous animals, 22, 23
Carroll, Lewis, 108
Carroll, Robert L., 17
Carson, Rachael, 113
Casteel, John L., 131, 163
Cave (Upper Paleolithic) men, 49–54
  group stability, 50
  unity with nature, 50–51
Caves, 31, 33, 42–43
Cenozoic era, chart, (42)
Center of gravity (psychological), 72, 141
Centrale (bone in wrist of amphibian, reptile, and mammal including apes, but not separate in man), 15
Centralized organs, chart stage 7
Centrosome, 10
Charisma, 98
Charity, 76, (88), **(89–90)**
Chastity, 151
Châtelperronian, 31
Chewing, rotary, 26
Child-adult genuine love relationship, **94–116**, 155, 160
Child of *Pithecanthropus*, 36
Chimpanzee, 27, 28, **36**, 61
China, 28, 29, 38, 59
Chins, 37, 41
Chlorophyll, 7–8, 9, 11n, chart
Chloroplasts, 8
Choanae, **14**, chart stage 10
Chopper-chopping tool cultures, 29
Chordates, 12, **13**, chart
Christian evidence of reality, **87**, churches, 151–152
Christian Scientists, 143, (152)
Christmas, spirit of, 106
Chromatophores, 10, 11n
Chromosomes, 9, chart
  sexual, 146

171

172

173

Eagles, 136
Ear, chart stage 11
Echinoderms, 13, chart
Eddington, Sir Arthur, 135, 163
Edentates, chart, 25
Education, 95–96
Eggs, laid on land, chart (stage 12), 18
Egocentricity, 43, **61–73**, 75, 82, 83, **88**, **89**, 93–94, 96, 98, 100, 106, 107, **124**, 125, 130, 138, 141, 142, 144, 149, **(154–155)**, **155–156**, **159**, 160, 161, 164
   interlocking reciprocal egocentricities, 69–71, 76, 77, 78, 79, 80, 81, 88, 99
Eidetic imagery, 52
Einstein, Albert, 137
Elections, 153–154
Electricity, 111, 142–143
Electromagnetic spectrum, 133, 143
Elizabeth, mother of John the Baptist, 146
Embalmed "we," 69
Embryonic stages, 12
Emotion, 150–151. *See also* Feelings
Empires, 60–61, 91
Empty House, parable, 90
Encouraging and harvesting wild plants, 44
Energy, biologic, 8, 11n, 13, chart, 21. *See also* ATP and metabolism
   higher order, 97
   physical, 133–135, 143
   psychological loss of, 71–72, 112, 126
England, 31, 32, 33, 35
Enlargement of consciousness or self. *See* Expansion
Enthusiasm for the universe, 46, 80, 99
   personal, 96, 97, 123, 156
Environment, biologic, 1
   changes in 1, 2, 28, 44
   childhood, 65–66
   deep-sea, monotonous, 12
   fresh-water, 13
   glacial, 18

marine, 4
return to ancestral, to raise young, 13, 16
surrounding, 16, 23, 46
varied, stimulating advance, 2, 8, 11n, 28
volcanic-lacustrine favorable for preservation, 33
Enzymes, 7
Eocene (epoch early in the Cenozoic), 25
Episcopal Church, 151
Epistemology, 135
Equality, 85–86, 157
Eryops, 15
Escapees, 69
Escuminac, Quebec, 15
Establishment, 154
Ether, 133
Ethiopia, 35 (twice), 41
Euglena, chart
Eukaryotes, 9, 11n
Europe, 18, 26, 31, 33, 35, 37, 38, 42, 43, 44, 58, 63
Eusthenopteron, 15
Eutheria, chart stages 15 and 16 on
Evil, origin of, 46, 149
Evolution of life, **chart**
   control of, ix, 1, 45, 47, *See also* Natural selection
   process of (or principles of, life relationships), **1–3**, 21–22, 23, 46–47, **64**, 154
Exaggeration, 153
Example to follow, Jesus as, 95, 146
Exclusiveness, 121
Excuses, 125
Expansion of consciousness, 137, 140–142, 147, 159, 165
Experience
   of genuine love, 73, 75, **76**, **77**, 78, 79, 80, 82, 85–86, (87), 88, 90, **91**, 93, 94, 116, 143, 153, 155, 160, 162, 164
   personal, iii, ix, 87, 94, 95, 100, 109, 162
   religious, 165
Exploitation, 43, (60–62), 68–69, **70**,

174

Helping, 47, 64–65, 68–71, 77, **80**, **82–83**, 89, 115–116, 152–153, 157
Henry, Marguerite, 108
Hens, parthogenetic, 146
Heredity, 7, 9, 145
Hero, heroine, 117
Heroic Age, 60
Hill, Cathy, 20, 22
Hips, **27**
History of life, vii, **ix**, **1–45**, 162
The History and Meaning of Life, 45
Hobby, 112, 122
Holes, or vacuities, in outer skull, by which reptiles are classified, 18, 19
Homer, 60
Hominoid, 26
Homo, chart (stages 20 and 21), 27, 29, **34**, 35
—*erectus*, (29), **(34)**
—*habilis*, (29)
—*modjokertensis*, 36
—*neanderthalensis*, **34**
—*sapiens, chart* (stage 21 only), **34**, 35, 43, 59. *See also* Man, modern type
Homosexuals, 157–158
Honesty, 115. *See also* Sincerity
Honorary grandparents, etc., 101
Hoofed mammals, chart, 25
Hormones, 143
Howells, Wm. W., 27, 164
Hoxne, Suffolk, England, 32
Humanities, vii
Humerus (upper arm bone), 15
Humility, 3, 79, 81. *See also* Meekness and Receptivity
Hungary, 31, 35
Hunting, 28, 39, 40, 44
Hyoid arch, chart stages 9 and 10
Hyomandibular bone, bracing jaw against brain case, 14, chart stages 10 and 11
Hypnotizing (or brainwashing) by T.V., etc., 70, 112

I's, 72, 132, 141
I-Thou attitude, 51, 79–80, 95

I-it attitude, 79, (84), (114)
Ichthyostega (from *ichthys*, fish, and *stage*, roofed), late Devonian amphibian intermediate between Crossopterygian fish (which see) and *Gephyrostegus*, a member of the *Labyrinthodonta* formerly known as the Stegocephalians ("roofed headed"), which evolved into many forms that had thick flattish skulls, the "boneheads of the late Paleozoic and early Mesozoic". *See also* Crossopterygian fish, Gephyrostegus
Ideals, 76, 95, 97
Ignorance (everybody's), 133–147
Illumination, 141
Illusions, 140, 144, 158
Impartiality, 76, 77, 79, (81), 82–83, (84), 85, 86, 91, 93, **119, 122,** (124)
Implements, 26, 28, 41, 44. *See also* Artifacts and names of cultures
Inaccuracy of social rules, 78, 106, **111**, 161
Incursions, 165
India, 28, 31, 32, 36, 141
Indigents, 154
Individualism, 46, **63–64**, 139–140, 142
Indulgence. *See* Self-indulgence
Industrial Revolution, 59
Inertia, 160, (162)
Infallibility, 141–142
Infants' and toddlers' modern developmental stages (psychological ontogeny), 49, 52
Infatuation, 129–130
Inferences, 133
Inheritance status, 128
Inheriting the earth, 23, 79
Initiative, 114
Innocence, 111
Inorganic soup, 5–6
Insanity, 63. *See also* Mental retardation
Insectivora, chart, 25

177

Insects, 14, 16
Inspirations, vii, 97, 117, 141, 146
Insurance companies, 134
Intangibles, vii
Integration, of scholastic disciplines, 152, 162
of selves, 141
of views in a controversy, 153
Integrity, 117
Intellectual consideration, 150
Intentions, good, 150
Interbreeding of different kinds of men, 38
Interest, all-round, 96, 112, 113, 115, 117, 125
Intermedium (bone in wrist of amphibian and reptile, below ulna between ulnare and radiale, corresponding to the mammalian lunar), 15
Intestine, 4, 12
Intimacy, complete sexual
reserved for all-round (adult) relationship, 108–109, 112, 117–118, 161
Should not be outstanding factor in marriage, 123
Intuition, 139
Invertebrates, 13, **chart**, 145
Iraq, 39–40
Isaiah, paraphrase of passage from, 148
Israel, 33, 34, 35, 38, 39. *See also* Palestine and Near East
Italy, 25, 26, 28

James, William, 141, 158, 165
Java, 29, 34, 36, 38, 59
Jaws, 14, chart (stages 8, 9, and 10), 19, 23, 26, 28, 29, 37, 41
Jealousy, 75, 80
Jebel Kafzeh, Israel, 35
Jesus, (76), 79, **87**, 88–91, 93, 94, 95, 101, 114, 127–128, 144, 145, 146, 147, 151, 155, 162
John, St., 77
John, St., of the Cross, 142
John the Baptist, 144, 146
Jointed, appendages, chart stage 7

central axes of fins, 14, chart stage 10
Joseph, 146
Joy in life, vii, 47, 73, 77, **80,** 90, 93, 97, 101, 113–114, 116, 124–125, **126,** 132, 140, 151, 155, 156, 159
Judeo-Christian evidence of reality, 76, **87**
Jung, Carl Gustav, 165
Justice in universal system, 139–140

Kanjera (East Africa), 35, 41
Keller, Helen, 157
Kelley, Thomas, 71, 165
Kidney, 11, 12, 13, chart (stages 6, 8, 12, 13A), **167**
mammalian, stage 13A, 19
uric acid, chart (among true reptiles and birds), 19, 21
Kindliness, 63, 156
Kingdom of God, or of Heaven, **87**, 93, 94, 105–106, 124, 140, 144, 147, 156
attainable now, 87, 90–91, 148–149
supreme importance, 87–88

Kingdoms (largest divisions of life), chart
King James version of Bible, 76
Kinship system, 54
Kipling, Rudyard, 108
Kissing, 110
Kropotkin, Petr, 165
Kunkel, Fritz, 49, 65, 69, 73, 165

labyrinthine teeth, chart stage 10
Labyrinthodonta (older amphibians), chart stage 11, **16**
laborers, 154
Laborers in the Vineyard, parable, 93
LaChapelle, France, 34
Laetolil (East Africa), 35
Language, see speech
Latimeria, chart, **16**
Leaders, religious and humanitarian, iii, 57, 76

group, 60, 125, 131

Leakey

    L. S. B., 165

    Mary, 30, 166

Learning from children, 95

Leaven, parable of, 90

Legal relations, 126

Legs, 14, chart stages 11, 13A, and (19), **15**, **27**, 33, 37

LeMoustier, France, 31, 36, 37

Lemurs, chart

Leucosin, 10, 11n

Lévy-Bruhl, Lucien, 51, 166

Lewis, C. S., 98–99, 105–106, 107, 108, 109, 166

Liberals, 63, 152

Licentious orgies, 62

Lichen, 8

Lieberman, Philip, 37

Life, in other parts of universe, 8, 47. *See also* Evolution, History, Origins

Limbs of higher vertebrates, 14, 15, 25. *See also* Legs

Lining up with the universe, vii, 46, 132, 149

Lips, chart stage 17

Lizards, chart

Lord's Prayer, paraphrase of, 148–149, 160

Lot's wife, allegory of, 88

Love

    child-parent, 98–99, 111

    of God and neighbor, 76–77

    genuine human, **45–46**, 55, 64, 72–73, **75–91**, 96, 99, 104, 105–106, 111, 112, 114, 122, **123–124**, **126**, 127, **128–129**, 138, 141, **142–143**, 144, 148–149, 151, **154–155**, 156, 157, 159, 160, 161, 164, 165

    from biologic roots, 95

    gift-love, 99

    imitations of, 70–71, 81–82, 118

    mother, 21, 50

    need-love, 98, 99

    improper uses of term, **76–77**, 97

    improper attempts to attain, **66–68**

Loyalty

    universal, 50, 60

    divided, 54–56

    a virtue, 60

    to modern group, 131

    to nominal marriage, 129

Lungs, 14, chart stage 10, 16

Lust, (61–62), 67, 81, 90, 96, 106, **111**, 112, (118), 121, 122, 126, 143, 158, 161

    romanticized, 76, 77, 78, 81, 86, 93

Lycaenops, **22**

MacDonald, George, 106–107, 166

Macromerion, 17

Macmurray, John, 150–151, 166

Madrasian-Stellenbosch culture, **31**, **32**

magic, 55–56, 57

main business of life, 76

main interest in life, 123, 156

main line of evolutionary advance, **2–3**, 4, 10, (**chart**), 19, 22, 25, 26, 45–46, 162

    characteristics of, **3**, 9–11, 42, 45

Mammals, **chart**, 21, 23, 25

    Mesozoic, 23–25

    very primitive, reptile-like, chart stage 13A, 18–20, 22, 26

Mammon, **89–90**

Man, 3, chart (stages 20 and 21), modern type, 27, 29, 33, 35, 36, 38, 40–42. *See also Homo sapiens*

Mana, 51

Marriage, (114), (118), **121**, (158), 160

    conventional or nominal, 123, 124–128, 129–130

    genuine, **123–124**, 126, 128–129

Marsupials, chart

Martha, 146

Mary, mother of Jesus, 146

Mary, sister of Martha, 146

Masculine dominance, 59–60

179

MAT (Mousterian of Acheulian Tradition), 40
Materialist, practical, 23
Maternal care, chart stage 13B, 21
Matter, solid, 133–135
    laws of, 134–135, 137
Mature "we," 73
Mauer jaw, 33
Meaning, in history of life, vii, 1
Mechanics, 142
Medieval times, 63, 156
Meditation, 72, 120, 125, 132, 140
Meekness, 3, 23
Meiosis, meiotic reduction in preparation for sexual union, 9, 11n, chart stage 4
Membrane, cell, 6, 7, 10, 145
    egg, 16
Men, 26, 28. *See also* Man
Mentality of modern primitives, 49, 51
Mesoderm (middle layer of multiplying cells, between inner and outer), 11, chart stage 6
Mesolithic, 44, 52
Mesozoic era, chart, 21, 23, 42
Metabolism
    oxygen, animal-like, 8, 11n, chart
    peculiar (anaerobic), chart
    photosynthetic, plant-like, 8, 11n, chart
    primitive ferments, 7, chart
Metal ages, 60, 62
Metazoan (multicellular animal), 9, chart stage 5
Micoquian, 32
Microliths, 44
Middle Stone Age, 44
Migrations, 26, 28, 31, 33, 44
Miller, Miss M. O., 31
Milne, A. A., 104
Mind, see consciousness and brain
Minority groups, 157
Miocene (epoch in early upper Cenozoic), 25
Miracles, 135–147
Mississippian (upper Paleozoic period after Devonian and before Pennsylvanian), 17

Mistakes, 25, 46
Mitochondria, 8
Mitosis (fully developed process of asexual nucleic division), 9, **10**, chart stage 4
Modjokertensis, Homo or *Pithecanthropus*, 36
Mohammedan Mosque, 152
Mohapatra, G. C., 32
Mollusca, mollusks, 13, chart
Monas, 11n
Money, viii, 88, 89–90, 97, 98
Mongoloids, 44
Monkey, chart (stage 18), 26, 52, 136
Monotheism, 62
Moon dances, 57–58
Montgomery, L. M., 108
Morality, 160–161
Mormon Church, 152
Morris, William, 108–109
Mosses (*Bryophyta*), 8, chart (left side). *See also* club mosses (Lycopods)
Mt. Carmel, Israel, 34, 38
Mousterian, **30–31**, 35, (38), 40–41
Multicellular organisms, 9, 11n, chart
Muscles, 11, 12, 13, 19, 28, 37
Music playing, 112, 122
Mustard Seed, parable, 90
Mystical participations, 50, 51
Mystery, viii–ix, 133–147
Mysticism, 140–142

Napier, John, 25
Natural selection, **1**, **16**, **19**, 26, (45–47). *See also* Evolution of life, process or principles of
Nature of ultimate reality. viii–ix, 46–47, 62, 76, 79–80, 87, 89
Neanderthal Man, chart stage 21, **34**, **35–40**, 41, 42, 43, 59
Near East, 38, 40, 44, 58, 60–61
Necrolemur, **24–25**
Nectonemertes, **12**
Neighbor, 77, 78–79
Nemertine worms (*Nemertea*), **9–11**, **12**, chart
Neolithic revolution, 44–45, 49, 52,

180

181

183

184

187

188